Compassion Fire

Birthing Purpose Out of Pain

Chavonda Thompson

WESTBOW
PRESS®
A DIVISION OF THOMAS NELSON
& ZONDERVAN

Editor
Linda Stubblefield, Affordable Christian Editing.

WestBow Press books may be ordered through booksellers or by contacting:

WestBow Press
A Division of Thomas Nelson & Zondervan
1663 Liberty Drive
Bloomington, IN 47403
www.westbowpress.com
1 (866) 928-1240

ISBN: 978-1-9736-7019-3 (sc)
ISBN: 978-1-9736-7021-6 (hc)
ISBN: 978-1-9736-7020-9 (e)

Library of Congress Control Number: 2019910227

Print information available on the last page.

WestBow Press rev. date: 9/12/2019

In Memoriam

In loving memory of my brother,
George (Lil George) Thompson, Jr.
May 14, 1983 – March 8, 2008

WORDS CAN'T EXPRESS how much we all miss you and love you! This is not the end but only the beginning. We will see you again soon—in just a little while. To God be the glory!

Acknowledgments

I DEDICATE THIS BOOK to You, Lord. You are first and foremost in my life. Through it all, You have been the constant in my life. You've guided me every step of the way. You're my everything! Thank You for trusting me with this task and for giving me the grace to complete it. I give You all the honor, praise, and glory for everything to which I place my hands. You bless it. This book is for Your glory!

To my parents, George and Gwen Thompson:

Words cannot express how much I love you both! I couldn't ask for better parents. You both are my biggest supporters, mentors, and intercessors. Everything that I am and that I have learned has been because of what you have both modeled to my siblings and me. My life is a result of the sacrifices you both made for your children. Thank you, Daddy and Mama, for always believing in me. I LOVE YOU!

To my son Xavier (Zay):

You're my heartbeat and my greatest inspiration. You're the reason why quitting wasn't an option. Everything I do is because of you! You are my greatest blessing—always have and always will be. Mama loves you, son!

To my sisters, Alishia and Evelyn:

I couldn't ask for better sisters than you two. We are so much alike in many ways, but yet so different! That's the beauty in having y'all as my sisters. We've shared so much of life together through thick and thin, through the rain and sunshine. We've been there for each other. I always look forward to our times of laughter together. I love y'all,

To my nieces and nephews:

I pray that you all will walk in the calling of God on your life at an early age and that you all will always be obedient to His leading. Your auntie loves y'all.

To my best friend-brother, Emmett Hathaway:

I can't put into words how much you mean to me. You've been a friend to me and a tremendous blessing in my life. I hold dear the words you've ministered to me, your prayers and words of encouragement. Thank you, mighty man of God! This book is a result of all your prayers. Thank you for pushing me!

ACKNOWLEDGMENTS

To Steven Jones:

Thank you for being a true friend to me. You've stood with me during some of the toughest and darkest times of my life. I am grateful and blessed to not only have you in my life, but to have you as a friend.

To DeAndre (Dre) Singletary:

Thank you for speaking this book out of me. I still remember meeting you for the very first time, and you prophesied about this book in me. That prophecy was four years ago, and the book has finally been birthed. Thank you for being a friend to me and for your obedience to God. Love you, brother.

To anyone else who held up my hands even for a moment while I wrote this book who I have failed to acknowledge, may I simply say thank you. I am grateful for every prayer, every phone call, and every word of encouragement sown into my life.

To God be the Glory!

Can we be touched by the hurt of humanity and not judge those who are hurting? Through a heart of compassion, we are able to help others to overcome that which we have overcome by the blood of the Lamb and the word of our testimony. We are overcomers.

Compassion

A mixed passion compounded of love and sorrow

A compassionate person has the ability to empathize with another's pain and suffering. Jesus was moved with compassion and healed all who were sick and afflicted (Matthew 14:14).

Fire

(n.) flame or heat, a state or process.

(v.) to apply heat

In the Bible, *fire* represented God's purity, presence and holiness. God appeared to Moses through a burning bush. The fire of God cleanses and purifies us. *"See I have refined you, though not as silver; I have tested you in the furnace of affliction"* (Isaiah 48:10).

Fire is a picture of the work of the Holy Spirit, the member of the Trinity who creates the passion of God in our hearts.

Table of Contents

My Testimony

I wasn't your normal every-day Sunday church goer. By that statement I mean my family primarily went to church during Easter and Christmas. However, I can still remember having to say Easter speeches for Easter at our family's home church and how my mama always made our Easter outfits.

We grew up very poor, but we had each other. What mattered to us is that we were family. I had amazing, loving parents who unconditionally loved their children. My dad grew up in church and always talked with us about Jesus, sharing stories and talking about the Word of God. I have many memories of always seeing him praying. Even though I knew about Jesus from my parents and from times of being in church, I did not know Him personally for myself; I did not have a personal relationship with Him until I got saved at the age of 24.

Prior to my being saved, I was living a life of nightclubbing, drinking, and engaging in sexual relationships with a few drug dealers. This lifestyle led to my getting pregnant at 21 years of age and subsequently undergoing an abortion. Several years later, I met my son's father and found myself pregnant at the age of 24. Being pregnant with my son Xavier was one of the best things that happened to me because I was forced to evaluate the life that I was living.

I knew my life was headed for destruction, but then I met a Savior named Jesus. I am not sure where my life would be right now if I had never surrendered my life to Jesus. From the path that my life was on, I know that I would probably be dead or serving real time in jail.

When I got saved, I truly got saved. I can still remember that day when I was at the altar and how I felt the presence of God and the love that He had for me. That love was so real to me that I cannot possibly explain in mere words. I knew in heart that my life was different from that point on; something radical had happened to me. I do not remember the date, but God knows. Who's to say that I am not saved because I cannot remember the exact date. I do think knowing the date is good, but if you cannot remember the actual date, don't allow anyone to disqualify you because of not knowing that date. Your salvation comes from God, not man, so how can a man decide whether or not you are truly saved. Salvation is through Jesus Christ alone. Period.

As I began to walk this journey with Christ, like anyone else, I experienced seasons of ups and downs. I realized that, through these seasons, my faith grew stronger as I learned more about His love, grace, mercy, compassion and how He wanted to use my story for His glory. Through our testimony we destroy the works of darkness and set the captives free. Through our testimony we are privileged to proclaim Jesus as the King of kings and Lord of lords. God has called me to be a deliverer because Jesus has delivered me to set free those who have been bound.

> Isaiah 61:1-3, *The Spirit of the Sovereign* Lord *is on me, because the* Lord *has anointed me to proclaim good news to the poor. He has sent me to bind up the brokenhearted, to proclaim freedom for the captives and release from darkness for the prisoners, to proclaim the year of the* Lord's *favor and the day of vengeance of our God, to comfort all who mourn, and provide for those who grieve in Zion—to bestow on them a crown of beauty instead of ashes, the oil of joy instead of mourning, and a garment of praise instead of a spirit of despair.*

CHAPTER ONE

What Do You Have?

I Kings 17:15-16

"As surely as the LORD *your God lives," she replied, "I don't have any bread—only a handful of flour in a jar and a little olive oil in a jug. I am gathering a few sticks to take home and make a meal for myself and my son, that we may eat it—and die." Elijah said to her, "Don't be afraid. Go home and do as you have said. But first make a small loaf of bread for me from what you have and bring it to me, and then make something for yourself and your son" – I Kings 17:12-13.*

T HE WIDOW WENT away and did as Elijah had instructed. As a result of her obedience, there was food every day for Elijah and for the woman and her family. Because this woman fulfilled Elijah's request and in keeping with the word of the Lord spoken by Elijah, the jar of flour was not used up and the jug of oil did not run dry.

———

_____

The land had been suffering from a severe drought because it had not rained for several years. God commanded Elijah to leave and go to Zarephath where a widowed woman would now feed him (I Kings 17:7-9). This widowed woman and her son were on the verge of starving to death. All she had remaining was a handful of flour and a little olive oil in a jug—barely enough to make a last meal for herself and her son (I Kings 17:12). Theirs seemed to be a hopeless situation, but Elijah instructed her to make him a meal first (I Kings 17:13).

Because the woman obeyed the instruction from the prophet Elijah, what she had was multiplied. What she had in her hands was her seed, and this seed released her breakthrough. The woman needed a miracle, and she gave out of obedience. What she needed was connected to her act of obedience. In order to test our obedience, God will oftentimes issue us an instruction that makes little to no logical sense. Obeying God puts us in a place of favor and will cause favor to follow us. Psalm 5:12 says that favor will surround us as a shield.

During the season of famine and drought, her jar of flour was not used up and her jug of oil did not run dry (I Kings 17:16). The very miracle she needed was already in her hands. Her story teaches that one act of obedience can change our circumstances. When the Supplier is God, not only can He sustain us during seasons of lack or not enough, but He can also make a way where there seems to be no way (Isaiah 43:19).

_____

WHAT DO YOU HAVE?

God is no respecter of persons; He does not show favoritism (Romans 2:11). What He did for the widowed woman and her son He can do for you. God will also honor your obedience. What do you need from God? Do you need a financial breakthrough or do you need healing? Whatever the need is in your life, know that God can provide exactly like He did for that widow woman because our God is no respecter of persons.

BLESSINGS FROM OBEDIENCE

Deuteronomy chapter 28 outlines the blessings of God for those who walk in obedience to His commands. Some of the blessings that will come upon those who are obedient include the following:

- You will be blessed in the city and blessed in the country.
- The fruit of your womb will be blessed, as will the crops of your land and the young of your livestock.
- Your basket and your kneading trough will be blessed.
- You will be blessed when you come and blessed when you go out.
- The enemies who rise up against you will be defeated before you.

- Your enemies will come at you from one direction but flee from you in seven.
- The Lord will send a blessing on your barns and on everything to which you put your hand.

The Bible is full of stories of those who trusted and obeyed God. The story of Abraham, the patriarch, tells of blessings from obedience. First, Abram was told to leave his country, his people, and his father's household to go to a land God would show him (Genesis 12:1-4). By faith Abraham, when called to go to a place he would later receive as his inheritance, obeyed and went—even though he did not know where he was going (Hebrews 11:8). Genesis 15:6 says that because Abraham believed God, his faith was credited to him as righteousness.

Later God tested Abraham and told him to sacrifice his only son Isaac. According to Genesis 22:3, Abraham did not waver in his faith as he rose early the next morning, loaded his donkey, and took with him two of his servants and his son Isaac. God is also moved by your faith. The Word of God says, "*Now faith is the substance of things hoped for, the evidence of things not seen*" (Hebrews 11:1 KJV). When we step out in faith, God will meet us right where we are, but we must put action behind our faith because faith without works is dead.

Obedience will always require action on your part. When we study and meditate on the Word of God, our faith grows.

After all, faith comes by hearing the Word of God (Romans 10:17). Hebrews 11:6 says that without faith it is impossible to please God. Each of us is given our own measure of faith; however, God is pleased when we have faith and put action behind it. James 2:22 says, *"You see that his faith and his actions were working together, and his faith was made complete by what he did."* Your faith and works go hand in hand. A person is considered righteous by what he or she does—not by faith alone (James 2:24).

Abraham was called away from everything with which he was familiar. He left what was familiar to him and stepped out in the unfamiliar. When God tells you to step out in faith like He did Abraham, He will not reveal the full blueprint of how the journey will look. The key is to take the first step—even when you don't know how His request will look. Only then can God begin to reveal your next step.

Trust me, I get it. Taking those steps can be scary—especially when it's unfamiliar to you. But friend, I would rather step out afraid then not step out at all. God has a plan and a destiny for every person's life that is good! He says in Jeremiah 29:11 that He knows the plans that He has for our life—plans that are for our good. Additionally, His plans are far greater than we can ever comprehend. I have many wonderful testimonies of God's faithfulness when I stepped out in faith—not knowing what the next step would look like.

As a Christian, our desire should be to fulfill all that the Lord has planned for our lives, leaving nothing undone when we leave this earth. Living a life of full surrender will require our trusting God even when we don't understand His leading. But trusting Him is not about our understanding His plans; rather, trust is about our being willing, obedient, and continually saying YES to God—no matter what that act of obedience looks like in the natural.

My writing this book was an act of obedience and faith to the One who spoke it in His plans even before the foundations of the world. The promises of God work by faith, and we must grab hold of them and begin to decree His promises over our life. When God speaks a word over our life, He watches over His word to perform it (Jeremiah 1:12). His promises are "Yes" and "Amen"; He is faithful to His word.

Oftentimes we are waiting for the next big event to happen in our lives, but God speaks to us about His plan for our life in the small and the simple—like a still small voice (I Kings 19:12). As a matter of fact, God is generally telling us what to do in the simple routine of day-to-day living that we tend to overlook. As I look back over my life and from what God has brought me, my journals are filled with stories of testimonies, victories, answered prayers, desires and dreams that God had given me. I never would have dreamed that God wanted to use my stories, but they were evidence of the hand of God on my life and His faithfulness to me in every season. He still continues to amaze me with His faithfulness—even at times when I wasn't so faithful. God helped me to process so many seasons through journaling.

After reading this story about Elijah and the widowed woman, I pondered the question, *"What do you have?"* The answer was simple: I had my journals. I realized they contained information that could be used to help someone else who could be going through the very same trials and tests that I had gone through. I knew God had placed the ball in my court, and He was waiting to see what I would do with what He had already given me.

So, my question to you is: *"What do you have?"* What gifts and talents do you have that can used for the kingdom of God? Take an inventory of your life and see what you enjoy doing. About what are you passionate? I have found what you are passionate about is usually a key to your gifts and talents. We have many ways of influencing others with our gifts and talents and by being a faithful steward and investing the resources He has given us will help influence others and also to continue to develop our gift.

Matthew 25:14-30 contains the parable of the talents and a master who entrusted his servants with a portion of his wealth. To one man he gave five bags of gold; to another, he gave two bags of gold; to another, he gave one bag of gold. The one who was entrusted with five bags immediately put his money to work for him and gained five more bags. The person with two bags of gold gained two more. But the man with the one bag was fearful, so he dug a hole in the ground and hid his master's money. When the master returned, he asked the man with one bag, "Why didn't you invest what you had? Why did you not use it in a way that would gain some interest?"

How does this parable apply to our life? Many times, we are hesitant to use our gifts and talents because we are afraid of being either rejected or misunderstood. Maybe we lack the complete wisdom and understanding in the matter or we simply don't know how to use them. Of course, a big reason is a fear of failure.

Whatever gifts and talents God has given us, we must use them for the glory of God! According to the grace extended to each of us, God has given each of us specific gifts (Romans 12:6-8). He doesn't want us to sit on it like the servant with the one talent and be an observer. Trust me, that's not God's will for our lives; He wants active participators in His kingdom. God has already equipped you, my friend, but you may be thinking that what you have seems too small or insignificant to be used for the kingdom of God. You must understand that there are no insignificant gifts or talents used for the glory of God. We have the tendency to overlook this truth. We see those who are on the platform or on the front lines, and we begin to think they have a greater gift or that God cannot use us because we are not gifted in that particular area. What a lie and trick of the Enemy who seeks to derail God's children!

First of all, we are not supposed to compare ourselves to each other. 2 Corinthians 10:12b (KJV) admonishes us, *"but they measuring themselves by themselves, and comparing themselves among themselves, are not wise."*

Secondly, we should not magnify the gift because it's not about the gift but about the Giver of the gift. There is no greater gift than the gift of salvation. Ephesians 2:10 says that we are His workmanship, created in Christ Jesus for good works, which God prepared beforehand so that we would walk in them.

Allow God to use what He placed inside of you and watch how He will begin to supernaturally increase what you have. Be like the boy who gave his sack lunch of five loaves of bread and two fish. God multiplied that lunch to feed over five thousand. You will be amazed how God will take what you already have in your hands and begin to multiply it when you give it to Him first.

My friend, you do not need to possess mountain-moving faith before you step out and do what God has called you to do. You need only faith the size of a grain of mustard seed. Do you know how big that faith is? A single mustard seed is one to two millimeters (.039-.079 inches) in size—about the size of two of the numbers on a penny! That mustard-seed-size faith is all you need to step out. Matthew 17:20b says, *"If you have faith as small as a mustard seed, you can say to this mountain, 'Move from here to there,' and it will move. Nothing will be impossible for you."* Begin to pray and ask God to show you what gifts and talents He has given you.

One of the greatest threats to a Christian believer is complacency. When God is stretching us, He will begin to call us out of our comfort zones. Sometimes our comfort zones can become like our security blanket, and as God begins to stretch us beyond our comfort zones, we tend to resist the urge to be stretched. My friend, do not resist the stretching; it is producing growth. The result of growth is fruit. Complacency also causes us to miss out on all that God has for us by keeping us stagnant. Anything that becomes stagnant is not growing, and anything that is not growing is not producing fruit.

Every Christian is called to be a fruit bearer for the kingdom of God. Satan uses stagnation against believers to keep them unproductive and ineffective for the kingdom of God. I have found that complacency is often rooted in the spirit of fear.

Revelation 3:15-16 strongly states that God prefers His children to be hot or cold instead of lukewarm. He will spew out lukewarm Christians. Who wants to drink a lukewarm cup of coffee or tea? God sees a Christian's being lukewarm like that cup of unpalatable lukewarm coffee or tea. A Christian who doesn't make use of his or her God-given gifts is lukewarm and distasteful to God.

Refusing to do what God has called us to do is disobedience.

God never called us to be an inactive Christian sitting on the sidelines. No! He called us to be active and effective for the kingdom of God. We cannot become pawns for the Enemy and allow him to make us fearful and ineffective for God's kingdom.

An ineffective, lukewarm Christian is no threat to Satan. The Evil One doesn't want us to witness to our co-worker or our neighbor about our faith; he doesn't want us praying for that single mom who maybe having a hard time. The Devil doesn't want us to invite anyone to church or to witness to others about our faith. No, our Adversary wants us to be fearful and doubtful about the things of God to keep us from moving forward and advancing His kingdom. Our taking action for God's work attracts Satan's attention, and he will do everything he can to hinder our service. We simply cannot give an ear to Satan and his lies.

The apostle Paul tells us in verses 10 and 11 of Ephesians 6 to put on the full armor of God so that we can stand against the wiles and attacks that Satan and his demonic forces launch against us. When we know who we are in Christ, the Enemy cannot intimidate us. With the armor of God, we can stand boldly for Him—no matter what the Enemy throws at us. My friend, determine in your heart and mind today that you will stand firmly for your faith no matter the consequences. This battle we are in is not about us; it's all about Jesus and what He did for us on Calvary. It's about spreading the gospel of Jesus Christ and saving souls for the kingdom of God.

One of my favorite stories in the Bible is about Peter's stepping out of the boat and walking on water. We read about Peter and his impulsive nature and sometimes risky behavior, but I love Peter's heart and his willingness to risk it all and step out on faith. If Peter would have stayed in the boat like the other disciples, he would never have experienced walking on water. Peter was willing to leave behind the familiar and step out into unfamiliar territory.

Have you ever noticed that Jesus did not rebuke Peter for stepping out when he started to sink? Instead, Jesus simply asked Peter, "Why did you doubt?" The issue wasn't at all about Peter's stepping out of the boat; Jesus focused on Peter's doubt, taking his eyes off Him, and looking at the storm. Peter's focus shifted from faith to doubt.

My friend, is God calling you to step out—like Peter did? Is He is calling you to step out on faith for that dream He has placed within you? Have you been afraid and, like the other disciples, have you been playing it safe by staying in the boat, so to speak? I don't know what God has called you to do, but don't sit on that dream one more day! Put feet to your faith. Change your focus from doubt to faith. It's time to move! Step out of the boat!

Are you willing to walk on water? Are you willing to step out on the things of God? If you have a yes in your heart, then it's time to go for it, friend. Peter only began to sink when he took his eyes off Jesus. As you step out into the unfamiliar, keep your focus and eyes on Jesus. Yes, you will have trying times, but God has people already in place who you are called to help. They are waiting on you to release what God has placed inside of you.

Saying yes is about obeying God and touching lives with our story. When we don't do what God has called us to do, we miss out on the very purpose that God has placed within us. We miss out on His best for our lives, and we don't live out our full potential. Oftentimes, making this mistake leads to our becoming frustrated and discouraged; we start to doubt the promises of God. We will begin to lose sight of the vision that God gave us, and if it is not birthed out, it will begin to die on the inside. We will miss out on that which God had intended for us to birth. That's why being in tune with the voice of God and the leading of the Holy Spirit is so important. If we are not, we can miss out on what God is saying and delay or forfeit our destiny.

Friend, please don't miss out on what God is telling you to do. Step out of the boat! I've been there myself, not knowing how to do what God told me to do. I have told God many times that I did not know how to do what He had called me to do, and He also knows you don't because you need Him to help you. For example, when God told Moses to go and speak to Pharaoh about releasing the children of Israel, Moses told God that he was not eloquent in speech to do what God had told him to do. God asked Moses, "Who made the mouth?" Like Moses, you may also have all kinds of excuses that come to your mind, telling you why you should not take that leap of faith, but no excuse will be valid with God. He knows exactly what He has placed on the inside of you and how He wants to use you to bring glory to His name, so no more excuses about why you can't.

If you have a vision from God, you cannot do it on your own; you will have to rely solely on God. This vision may require your being misunderstood by those who don't or won't understand your calling or assignment. Your vision may require you to walk through a lonely season of sacrifice through prayer, fasting and reading the Word of God. Your vision from God may require your giving up some of your enjoyable pastimes during that season in order to draw closer to God so you can clearly hear His voice. Oh, but the joy of that "baby" when it has been birthed and the lives you will change through your obedience.

One of the first steps is to prepare for where you are going. Preparation requires diligence and action. When you are diligent about a project or a vision, you are in persistent pursuit. Many times, we sit waiting on God, but God is waiting on us to step out. He wants to be believed. He wants us to take Him at His Word. He wants us to ask for the things that only He can do because He gets the glory for our lives when we trust Him and take Him at His Word. His Word is everlasting. Think about it! The God who spoke creation into existence wants to use you and me. How awesome and exciting is that? We have the privilege of participating in the plans of God!

WHAT'S IN YOUR HANDS?

In Exodus 4:2, God asked Moses what he had in his hand. Moses had a staff. What he needed to help deliver the children of Israel from Pharaoh was already in his hands. God told Moses to stretch out his hands, and as Moses obeyed, the Red Sea was parted. Like Moses, everything you need from God, you already have. He has already equipped you for the task. He has given you the ability to do what He has called you to do. God is waiting on you to act. Sometimes we fail to realize is that the very thing we are waiting on God to perform, He has already placed in our hands! By faith, Moses used what God had placed in his hands to bring about deliverance for the children of Israel.

Gideon saw himself as insignificant and incapable of doing what God had called him to do. But God called him a "mighty man of valor." God calls us by how He sees us—not by how we see ourselves. Gideon was fearful about stepping out, so he asked God for confirmation by laying out his fleece before God. We can all be like Gideon at times and "fleece" God when He tells us to step out and we are unsure if we heard Him correctly. We want confirmation after confirmation before we finally step out.

As a baby learns how to walk, he or she will need assistance.

Like a baby is how we are in our faith walk. When we are a babe in Christ, we may need the security of having confirmation after confirmation like Gideon, but as we mature in our relationship with Him, we should recognize His voice and leading when He instructs us. Obey the first time He speaks!

Perhaps you are at a point of frustration with some matters in your life and you want more of God, but you seemingly cannot break through. Could it be the reason you are frustrated is because you have not done what God clearly instructed you to do? God will begin to frustrate *your plans* so that you will step out on what He has told you to do.

Frustration will cause you to move and can help birth what's on the inside of you. When directed positively, the dissatisfaction of frustration can be a catalyst behind prayer that will help propel you forward into your destiny. You might be saying, "How do I know what God is telling me to do is of Him?"

Does the instruction line up with the Word of God? Will following His instructions advance the kingdom of God? Has what you believe He has spoken to you left you? It won't leave you; you will always be thinking about what He wants. God will give you a burden for the assignment He has called you to do. You will not have true peace and contentment in your life until you are doing what God has called you to do. I often see so many people every day who are dissatisfied with their lives and their jobs. Sadly, the primary reason is because they are not living out their dreams, so they live unfulfilled and frustrated with their lives. God wants us to enjoy life; His Word says in John 10:10 that He came so that we can have life and life more abundantly. The only way we can live a fulfilled life is to walk in our purposed calling that God has for us.

THE MALACHI MANDATE

According to the *Cambridge Dictionary,* a *mandate* is "an official order or commission to do something; an instruction, a directive, a decree or a command."[1] One way to experience increase in your life is to become a tither. The Bible commands us to tithe in Malachi 3:10, which says:

> *"Bring the whole tithe into the storehouse, that there may be food in my house. Test me in this,"* says the LORD Almighty, *"and see if I will not throw open the floodgates of heaven and pour out so much blessing that there will not be room enough to store it."*

God doesn't need our money, but God uses money as a tool to accomplish His plan on earth. When we begin to have financial stress, we tend to want to hold on to what we have out of fear, but this is the time to continue to be faithful to God through tithing and giving offerings.

Oftentimes, we want God's blessing, but we don't want to be obedient to the mandate of Malachi 3:10. Sorry, my friend, but God doesn't work that way. Yes, God wants to bless us, but God has set biblical principles in place to receive His blessings, and tithing is one of them. This Scripture is the only one where the Lord tells us to *test* Him. God says what He will do in Malachi 3 if we will obey this principle:

1) He will open the floodgates of heaven over our life with so much blessing that there will not be room enough to store it (v. 10).

2) He will prevent pests from devouring our crops, and the vines in our fields will not drop their fruit before it is ripe (v. 11).

3) All nations will call us blessed, and we will have a delightful land (v. 12).

As we remain faithful to God and His Word, we will begin to see God's blessings begin to chase us down. *"Give and it shall be given unto you; good measure, pressed down, shaken together, and running over, shall men give into your bosom…"* (Luke 6:38).

The Enemy does not want the child of God to obey this principle because he knows the spiritual blessings connected to obeying this verse. The Enemy wants every child of God to remain ignorant to the promises of the Word of God and not know the benefits of obeying God's Word. If he can keep a believer from tithing, he can keep that person in financial lack and bondage. But God's will is for every child of God to live a life of abundance instead of living from paycheck to paycheck and barely making a living.

No, I am not talking about obtaining material possessions; rather, I am referring to living a life of abundance in every facet of our life—spiritually, financially, physically and emotionally. God came so that we can have life and life more abundantly (John 10:10). The key to living the abundant life is in obeying God's Word and His principles.

When I first became a Christian and learned about the principle of tithing and the spiritual blessings connected to giving, I remained faithful in my tithing and offering to my local church and to the kingdom of God. And as a result of my obedience, I have seen God supernaturally provide for my son and me—like He provided for the widowed woman and her son during a season of famine and drought. I watched as God multiplied what I had because I gave to Him first.

One of the names of God is *Jehovah-Jireh* which means "the Lord will provide" (Genesis 22:14). God is faithful, and we can trust Him to provide everything we need. Whether your needs are physical, spiritual, financial, emotional or relational does not matter. He can and will provide for you all you have to do is trust and obey His Word.

Questions

1) What do you have? What gifts or talents has God placed on the inside of you that you have been hesitant to step out and use?

2) When was the time you stepped out in obedience to God on an instruction that He gave you? And what blessings have you reaped from obeying?

3) What has God placed in your hands that can be used to impact and influence lives around you for His kingdom?

4) How have you seen God provide for you by obeying the principle of tithing?

---

1   "Mandate," Cambridge Dictionary, https://dictionary.cambridge.org/us/dictionary /english/mandate.

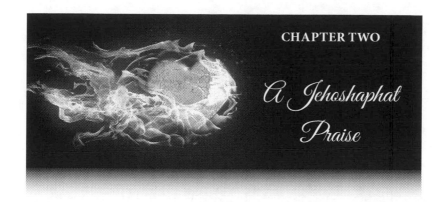

CHAPTER TWO

A Jehoshaphat Praise

Do not be afraid or discouraged because of this vast army. For the battle is not yours, but God's. ¹⁷You will not have to fight this battle. Take up your positions; stand firm and see the deliverance the LORD will give you. Do not be afraid; do not be discouraged. Go out and face them tomorrow and the LORD will be with you. – 2 Chronicles 20:15b, 17

JEHOSHAPHAT SENT "PRAISERS" ahead of the army, and the battle shifted. Praise shifts the atmosphere every time. If you want to see victory in your situation from your enemies, simply begin to give God praise in the midst of your battle and watch Him bring victory to that situation. That those to give praise were sent out ahead of the army is of importance to note. As they began to sing, the Lord set ambushes against the men of Ammon and Moab and Mount Seir who were invading Judah, and as a result, they were defeated (2 Chronicles 20:22).

Their uplifting praise shifted the battle in their favor against their enemies.

Every time you begin to praise God, your praise sends confusion to the Enemy's camp. You may be going through a difficult season right now where it seems as if you are outnumbered and surrounded by the enemy. May I encourage you to take your eyes off your circumstance and begin to praise God?

The Enemy may think that he has you surrounded on every side, but do not be afraid or discouraged because the battle is not yours; it is the Lord's. The victory is already won. More are with you than are against you (2 Kings 6:16). You are surrounded by the army of the Lord; a heavenly host of angels are encamped around you. You must remember that yours is a "fixed" fight, and the battle has already been won on Calvary! Therefore, you are not fighting *to* victory, but *from* victory. It's not about your circumstance; rather, it's about a God who is bigger than what you are facing! You may not feel like praising God right now, but this trial is not about how you feel. You may be in despair and feel as though you do not have anything else left in you to give, but the best time to give God a sacrificial praise is right now in spite of your circumstance. There is power in your praise. Glory to God!

Satan already knows the power of praise; that's why he doesn't want you to praise God. Praise and worship disarms

Satan and his works, reminding him of when his heavenly job was praising God—before he was kicked out for his pride. Luke 10:18 says, *"I saw Satan fall like lightning from heaven."* Praise takes the very thing that he meant for your harm and turns it around for your good. When the Enemy hears your praise, he runs! Begin to praise and worship God and watch the Devil flee. It's time to praise your way out of defeat, discouragement, fear, depression, and debt. God has already given you the victory for this battle, and it's in your praise.

AUGUST 29, 2005

My parents had been staying with me for two weeks until some repairs and remodeling had been made to their house. Just before they returned to their home, Hurricane Katrina hit. The water was over the eight-foot mark in their house, and if they had stayed, they could have drowned. We were grateful to God that none of our family members were hurt and that we were together.

For the next several weeks, the American Red Cross brought us hot meals to eat. We had no transportation to go anywhere, and almost everything within a certain radius was devastated. We looked forward to seeing the volunteers with the Red Cross, who helped so many people during this time of great need. They may never know the full impact they made on our lives and our community. We were so grateful to those who faithfully served us hot meals every day. How much we take for granted every day is amazing.

Over the next several weeks, repairs began slowly, and we finally had hot water and electricity. We now felt less like we were living in a developing nation! During times of waiting like this, you see the strength and unity of your community. Churches were at the forefront of helping and serving the area in every way possible. I was happy to see that my local church had sustained only minimum damage as the building had been constructed on a slight incline. My pastor always had a heart for serving outside the church walls through community outreach and evangelism. Katrina did not stop us from continuing to reach out. Our church, along with many others, went into immediate action, serving and helping to rebuild our city.

The next step was to find some place for us to sleep. We soon received assistance from FEMA with our living conditions. Camper trailers were delivered, and my parents received approval to have one pulled on their property. They would live in this small FEMA trailer for nine months while their house was being gutted and rebuilt. There was barely enough room for my parents and youngest sister who was pregnant with my nephew at the time in that small cramped FEMA camper trailer.

Despite the cramped and uncomfortable living conditions, my parents made it work by always seeing the brighter side of the situation. My dad, who is known for being the most encouraging at the worst of times, always had a different perspective because his hope was in God. Growing up, my dad's tremendous faith in God is what held us together as a family. Two of his oft-repeated sayings, "Things could always be worse" or "Things never stay the same" have always given me hope during some of my toughest times. I have watched my parents endure some very hard times, and looking back over my life, I can say that I got my tremendous faith and strength from both of them.

Thankfully, my parents were some of the few who had invested in flood insurance. You would logically think with living so close to the Gulf of Mexico that more people would have purchased that coverage. However, no one was prepared for or expecting the massive amount of water that Hurricane Katrina unleashed on the coastal area. I continued to live in my apartment while the repairs were completed. Our building damage was minimal compared to what some others sustained.

After Katrina, I did not return to college. Instead, I accepted a job with FEMA, which was contracted through a job working at a local community action center. Our primary goal was helping to rebuild our community by assisting those who qualified for appliances such as refrigerators and stoves. This assistance was really aimed at helping the elderly community and those within a certain income bracket to receive help. When the contract with FEMA finally ended, I did not know where I would continue to work since jobs were still scarce.

My sister Alishia had been urging us to relocate to Knoxville, Tennessee, to start over. After months of considering her offer and much prayer, I had peace about moving. A big plus was the fact that my sister and her family were there already. At least I would have family and I would not be alone in a new place. So, I packed all our belongings in a U-Haul, and my dad hired U-Haul drivers to deliver my belongings. Xavier and I rode the greyhound bus over fourteen hours from Mobile, Alabama, to Knoxville, Tennessee. I can remember seeing the mountains in the background as we traveled through them. Those beautiful mountains almost seemed like they had been painted on a canvas. I had never seen anything like them. I thought they were just so beautiful.

Stay Praising ME

On December 19, 2007, my son and I finally arrived in downtown Knoxville at the Greyhound bus station after 4:00 in the morning. I was exhausted after the long ride, but at the same time, I felt great excitement at the joy of seeing my brother-in-law waiting to pick us up. I had missed my sister Alishia, my brother-in-law, and my niece Aniyah who I lovingly called "Nookie." They had moved to Knoxville months after Katrina in 2005. They had now been living there for two years.

A Jehoshaphat Praise

As I took in the atmosphere, I felt we had made a good choice. Moving to a new place with better opportunities and a new beginning felt good. I could hardly wait to see what God had in store for us. *The sky's the limit,* I thought. Even though I was a small-town country girl, I always had big dreams. Alishia and my brother-in law helped me with navigating around the area. I quickly found and settled into an apartment and started learning my way around, which didn't take that long. In comparison to my small hometown, navigating downtown Knoxville felt as if I was in New York City! I laugh now, thinking about how big I thought Knoxville seemed at the time. Not long after getting settled, I started looking for a church for us to attend. Finding a church home was of the utmost importance to me.

Knoxville has many churches from which to choose, and I noticed there almost seemed to be a church on every corner. I soon found a great local church and started attending with my son. When I moved to Knoxville, I already had a job offer with CVS Pharmacy, and I was in training as a traveling pharmacy sales associate. The job helped me to learn the area even more quickly as I was required to travel locally to different CVS locations to fill in when needed.

I was on the job a little over two months when I received an unexpected call from my mama on March 8, 2008. I had just arrived home from work, and the American Red Cross had called my parents to inform us that my brother George had been involved in an accident on the USS *Theodore Roosevelt*.

The information we were given made his injury sound minor. Shortly after getting off the phone with my mom, I called my dad. I vividly remember telling my dad, "Everything is going to be okay," but I could sense that my dad knew something was wrong.

Within hours, I received another call from my mother. I could hardly make out what she was saying as she tried to talk through her sobbing. She finally gained some control, and then I heard her say, "He's gone, Chavonda. Lil George is gone."

Her words shook me to the core. I couldn't wrap my mind around what she had just said. A flood of emotions hit me all at once. I felt as though my heart had stopped beating and as if I had an out-of-body experience. I couldn't breathe and began fighting for every breath. My head begin to swim, and everything began to feel small—as if I was suffocating. I didn't know what to do; I remember feeling like running. I collapsed on my living room floor and laid there unable to move from the weight of the pain.

Within seconds of hanging up the phone with my mother, my sister called Alishia, and I heard more screams of agony on the phone. *God, please help us!* was all I could think about or say! *This cannot be real! This moment feels so unreal.* I jumped in the car with Xavier and rushed to my sister's apartment where

I found her crying and pacing outside. Her husband was at her side, trying to console her.

The Navy had sent chaplain officers to deliver the news. My mom was alone at her house when they delivered the news about my brother. My dad was a second-shift worker at that time. When the military shows up wearing their dress white uniforms, you know they are delivering bad news. The days and weeks following that visit now begin to run together in my mind. Time seemed to stop with the news of my brother's untimely death. Xavier and I stayed at my sister's place the rest of that night. We couldn't sleep that night as we took turns holding each other and talking to our family. My youngest sister Evelyn had been closest to my brother as they were practically like twins. Hearing her stricken sobbing voice on the phone, repeatedly asking me why, knowing I was almost 600 miles away from her, and knowing that I couldn't be with her to comfort her was almost too much for me to bear. We decided to leave early the next morning to go home to our family.

The nine-hour drive back home that day seemed to be the longest drive home ever. We couldn't seem to get home fast enough, and I was averaging between 85 and 90 miles per hour. At that time, my mind wasn't concerned about being stopped by police. I was simply trying to get home. When we arrived, my parents were surrounded by extended family, including my dad's two oldest brothers and one of my mom's sisters. Alishia and I rushed through the door, grasping for our parents and holding tightly to them.

Mom sat in a corner chair with her hands gently folded in her lap, not saying a word. My dad stayed busy, trying to hold it together for all of us at the same time. My heart couldn't take it; I was hurting so bad. My dad and my brother had always enjoyed a close bond. Dad had always called him "a soldier," and that's what he had become. He served as a soldier here on earth, but now he had advanced to becoming a soldier in the heavenly army of the Lord.

For days and even weeks we were surrounded by visiting family and friends who wanted to pay their respects and help console us during this time of grief. The local news interviewed my family and did a segment and tribute to my brother for his service to our country.

We were finally given the details of my brother's "injury." While he was on the flight deck, a massive wave seemingly out of nowhere had hit the ship, violently slamming George into a hinged steel door and washing several others overboard. He sustained a severe head injury. My parents asked for an autopsy to be performed. The medical examiner confirmed that he had sustained a tremendous blow to the head, fracturing his skull and taking his life.

The chaplain who had been assigned to our family helped us through the whole ordeal. He informed us that the Navy report stated my brother had died in the transporting helicopter off the coast of Florida en route to the nearest hospital. My parents received the full detailed report from the Navy about the incident. To this day I have never read that report, and I do not know if can ever bring myself to read it.

I was still relatively new with the CVS Pharmacy, and my employers were generous for allowing me the extended time to be with my family. I believe God gave me favor with my job during this time, and I was able to stay a month with my parents. When the time came for Xavier and me to return to Knoxville, I could barely think about going back. I honestly wanted to quit my job and move back home to be with my parents. However, my parents assured us that returning to work and getting Xavier back in school was right to do. I didn't know how well I would function upon returning to work or what my job performance would be, but I did know my life would never be the same. If I had not had a sister in Knoxville, I do not know if I would have made it through those days. Alishia and I were there for each other, helping and encouraging one another, pulling each other through the coming days.

Some days were better than others though no words could adequately express the pain we felt at times. We had always been close as a family, so we talked with each other regularly. As the months passed, we frequently traveled home to be with my parents. Each time I visited, I felt the strong presence of the Lord dwelling in their house. Without a shadow of doubt, I knew God was there comforting and ministering to my parents in such a real and tangible way that His presence in their home was undeniable.

Even though I desperately wanted to move back home to be with my parents and my youngest sister Evelyn, I knew God had them in His hands. When the time came to leave for Knoxville, my dad never liked to see us leave, which made leaving even harder, He would always ask, "Could you just stay one more day?" My brother's death made saying goodbye even more difficult for us.

Our family always enjoyed being together, laughing at silly things and reminiscing about past times. In late August of 2008, five months after my brother's passing, I decided to enroll in the University of Tennessee. God gave me favor with the admissions department recognizing me as an in-state resident, enabling me to pay in-state tuition fees instead of an out-of-state tuition rate. I had always wanted to return to school since I had been unable to finish my degree at the University of South Alabama after Katrina. I had never had the opportunity to graduate from high school. I earned my GED after being expelled from school in eleventh grade for fighting. I had finally endured enough bullying and stood up for myself.

Up until that point I had never been in any trouble at all. I was never a bully or a problem kid. I was loner who was always very quiet. When the assistant principal talked to my parents, he basically informed them that he did not even know of me prior to this incident because I was never in any kind of trouble. In my first fight at school, I was handcuffed by a police officer and escorted off the school campus and seated in the back of a police cruiser. I was then taken to jail. I had only been there ten minutes when I saw my parents arrive and wait in the lobby. Of course, they had to wait for me to be processed, fingerprinted, and my mugshot taken. After the processing was completed, I was released on bail.

My parents quickly approached me to ask, "Are you okay? What happened?"

"I was tired of the bullying."

My parents had to come up with the money to retain a lawyer to defend me and to try to keep me in school which was another added stress. The school system expelled me for a year. I also had to appear in court. Ultimately, I was fined and placed on probation, though I no longer remember how long. All I know is that I greatly regretted all the pain and heartache my parents suffered with trying to keep me in school. Instead of being behind a year and dealing with all the humiliation, I decided not to return to school. I began studying for my GED, and I had to take it a couple of times to pass. Unfortunately, I had no plans about what I wanted to do. I had not learned any trade nor did I have experience or expertise in any area that would qualify me for a better job. I thought about joining the military but soon changed my mind.

I wanted to provide a better living for myself and my son, but I wasn't sure if I had the endurance and strength for the long haul. I was still trying to regain my strength from mourning. Grief completely saps the mind and body of energy. I was so tired of being on welfare and government assistance because of the many required appointments and meeting so many guidelines to get the help.

For all the critical people who judge those who legitimately need help or assistance from the government in order to provide for their family, please know some people genuinely need the help and are not "riding the system." They are trying their best. I was working full-time and attending school full-time, but my income wasn't sufficient to pay rent, daycare, food, gas, and my other necessary bills.

We can become so judgmental and self-righteous when judging someone without knowing his or her full story. If you have no knowledge of what they have had to face to get to this point, then you have no right to judge. Unless you have walked a day in their shoes, don't speak down about people who receive assistance. I always say, "Be careful how you criticize someone because you may find yourself in that same situation." If you have never had to stand in a welfare line, then thank God for the better living situation you have. Better yet, quit judging others who have to in order to survive and to provide for their family. I can assure you that most don't want to be on assistance in the first place. I desired a better life for us, and I knew it was coming soon. I simply had to endure through college—even though it was hard for me. I had to work hard at studying and keeping my mind focused.

STAY PRAISING HIM

Even though attending college gave me a focus for the future, some days were better than others. One of those days came when it seemed as if I could not take one more step forward. I had been dealing with depression and heavy grief—so much so that I did not know if I could make it to see the next day. I was already taking a low dosage of antidepressants, and if I managed to get up each morning and place my feet on the floor, that was a good day of making progress. As I was lying on my bedroom floor with tears streaming down my face, I can remember God's saying to me in His still small voice, "Stay praising ME." Until that moment, I know I had nothing left in me. To say I was tired was an understatement. I have learned that grief has a way of completely zapping every ounce of strength from within you, but as I begin to lift my hands right there and praise God, He begin to flood me with His presence. Our praise is never about us; it's all about the One who is worthy of our praise.

Praise takes your eyes off your circumstance and places

your focus on the One who is bigger than your circumstance. Praise and worship start at the beginning of church services for a reason; it sets the atmosphere for the presence of God. Psalm 22:3 says that God inhabits the praises of His people. The word *inhabit* means "to live or dwell in a place." Your praise will always attract the presence of God.

Our praise should not be solely reserved for Sunday morning; we should live a lifestyle of praise because praising magnifies our God over our problems. I'm not being unsympathetic about what you may be facing or going through; trust me, I understand. I have been where you are. I've had my share of painful seasons to walk through, and when we are going through a crisis, I know the last thing you want to do is praise God. I had to learn that what I was going through was the best time to praise Him. Praising God when everything is going good in your life is easy, but can you praise Him when your world is rocked? When the doctor gives you a bad report, when a close friend betrays you, when your job is terminated, when your spouse files for a divorce, or when a loved one is taken, can you praise Him? Yes, these situations can be extremely traumatic, but we should never lose our praise!

The hardships and trials of life should be opportune times to praise God. These times are a test of a true worshiper's heart. True worship is to worship God in spirit and in truth (John 4:23-24). We worship God based on the truth of who He is in spite of what we are going through. I don't know what you may be facing or going through right now, but if you will continue praising God in this situation, you'll see your circumstance begin to change.

Worship is not so much about the position, but about the posture of the child of God's heart. Christians desperately need to realize the power that lies in their praise. Praise is a weapon of warfare against the Adversary, which is why the Enemy wants to do nothing more than to steal your praise. If he can get you to stop praising God, then you'll begin to magnify your circumstance with worry, fear and doubt. He wants you to align yourself with him and his works.

When reading about the life of David, we can see how he lived a life of worship. David was a worshipper, which may be why the Scripture says that David was a man after God's own heart. Many of the Psalms, which were penned by David, tell how he endured many trials of life, but in every circumstance, he continued to praise God.

Acts 16:25-26 tell how Paul and Silas were praying and singing hymns to God at the midnight hour. The other prisoners were listening to them when a violent earthquake shook the foundations of the prison. All the prison doors flew open, and every prisoner's chains came loose. Paul and Silas were singing and praising God at a time when it seemed darkest. Like their praises set them free, your praise could be the very thing that sets others free. When you hold onto your praise, you are hindering the Spirit of God from flowing. Who knows but what your praise could be a point of deliverance for someone!

Someone else may be bound without the freedom you have to praise God, but your praising God could set that person free. Your praise may not be like someone else's praise, but who cares. No one is concerned about what your praise looks like. Your praise is your praise! I can tell you that I absolutely love to get caught up in praise and worship. Even the rock and all of creation cries out in praises to Him regardless if we fail to praise God (Luke 19:40). That verse tells us that all of creation is created to praise God and to tell about His goodness; therefore; we should never hold onto our praise. We should always be willing to tell others about the wonderful things that God has done in our lives.

HANG IN THERE

As I neared the end of my studies, I thought about quitting several times. I was weary and discouraged, and all the hours of studying had taken a toll on me. Plus, no matter how hard I tried, I could not pass two courses that I would repeat three times. Thankfully, my parents constantly encouraged me and held up my arms when I thought I couldn't continue.

My dad, who is one of the strongest people I have ever known, would not let us quit at anything. When things got tough for me, he would say, "Hang in there." I also reminded myself that having a better life for my son was my reason for not quitting. I had never let Xavier quit when things got tough, so why would I even consider quitting on him? Even though I thought about quitting, something inside of me wouldn't let me. Because I was so determined and persistent, I continued to battle on despite the hardship. In my final year of school, I worked hard to master those two classes that I had to repeat.

After I completed my finals, I anxiously waited for the grades to post. When they finally posted, I couldn't believe that my persistence had paid off. I had passed those two classes! I was finally graduating after five long hard years of college at UT. Xavier was so excited when I told him I would be graduating. After all, he had sacrificed along with me on this journey, so I felt I wasn't earning that degree alone; my son had earned it with me. My parents drove up for my graduation, and on December 13, 2013, when my name was called, I walked across the platform of the Thompson-Boling Arena to receive my degree. Tears were in my eyes, and my hands were raised in the air, giving God all the praise and glory for Jesus alone had brought me through those hard years.

You may be in a similar situation; you're weary from the journey and tempted to quit. Please don't! May I encourage you to continue on? All things come to an end as will this season you are experiencing. When I read the following quote, I was blessed and want to share it with you: "Winners are willing to do what losers won't." In order to win at anything, you must be determined to persevere through the hardships of life. You must be willing to go the extra mile when others refuse in order to reach your destination.

This journey that you are on is bigger than you. You're not simply doing this for yourself; you are doing this for others. When you refuse to quit or give up, you may be the trailblazer or forerunner in your family to break off the generational curses on your bloodline. The truth is that generational curses on your family are the reason why the journey has been so difficult. The Enemy has sought to stop you from moving forward by throwing everything he can your way.

Instead of succumbing to his plans, continue to stand on the promises of the Word of God and keep fighting the good fight of faith. You may have to fight with tears rolling down your face but keep throwing blows at the Enemy. Don't you dare lie down and quit! Don't you dare give up! You have come too far to throw in the towel. Yes, you will make it through this struggle in life. And when God delivers you, you will be able to deliver others. Moses was called to be the deliverer for the children of Israel, but God did not use Moses to help deliver the nation until He delivered him first. My friend, because you are also a deliverer, this path has not been easy for you. God cannot use

---

you to deliver others until He delivers you from your personal struggle.

Our life is a walking testimony of the faithfulness of God. We can praise God for many things, and the very fact that you have breath in your lungs and are reading this book means that God still has a plan for your life—a plan that is good. His plan is not by happenstance or coincidence; rather, His plan is a divine appointment ordained by the One who loves you.

Questions

1) What has praise and worship taught you?

2) Has there ever been a time or a season in your life where you found it hard to praise God?

3) How has praise and worship brought you through of some of your hard seasons?

CHAPTER THREE

Not the Scenic Route

A Wilderness Experience

When Pharaoh let the people go, God did not lead them on the road through the Philistine country, though that was shorter. For God said, "If they face war, they might change their minds and return to Egypt." ¹⁸So God led the people around by the desert road toward the Red Sea. The Israelites went up out of Egypt ready for battle. – Exodus 13:17-18

G OD DID NOT lead the Israelites on the shorter route in the wilderness because He knew if they had faced the Philistines in battle, His people would have been afraid and would have returned to bondage. God does not always take us via the easy way. He knows what lies ahead of us on our path. Even though God could have led the Israelites on the shorter route, which should have only taken eleven days; instead, the journey took them forty years. God knew that facing the Philistines in battle would have led them back to bondage.

The Philistines were a much stronger people than the Israelites, and up until that point, they had never had to face war of any kind. Because of the children of Israel's disobedience and rebellion, God led them to wander through the wilderness for forty years. You may be on the backside of the mountain and wondering, *why isn't a breakthrough forthcoming in our lives?* It may seem like you have been in a dry season longer than you expected, but the good news is that your wilderness season will not last forever.

When we think of a wilderness, we tend to think of desolate, barren, and dry; and in some cases, this description fits how our life may seem spiritually. We often equate a wilderness season to being under God's judgment, but this reasoning is not always correct. Your being in a dry season is not necessarily related to God's displeasure. Whatever the reason, this season should be a time of drawing closer to God, which is oftentimes the case when we go through a wilderness season. When our life seems spiritually desolate, God may be trying to get our attention to tell us the time has come to get away for a while. I believe the word *solitude* perfectly describes this time alone with God.

If you have ever been through a wilderness season, you probably wanted this season to conclude as quickly as possible, but you have to trust that God knows what He is working in you. Your faith will be tested greatly as a season of desolation can be a painful time for some because it seems as if God has abandoned them. You may even feel out of place and off balance at the same time. However, our loving God uses this time to help train and prepare us for where we are going. Our wilderness season is your training season.

I've learned to embrace my wilderness season—not run from it—because I know God is doing His greatest work in my life. I cannot testify to the fact that I have liked those seasons because in all honesty, I have not. However, I have learned to yield and submit to what He is teaching me during this time. Yes, God is seemingly silent during this time but consider this: the teacher is always silent during the test. Even though I may have felt like He had abandoned me, the truth is He never left me because He promises He will never leave us. Staying in faith and keeping the right perspective during these tough seasons is important.

The Enemy wants to capture your focus during your time of wilderness, and his desire is for you to take your focus off God. Ignore the Evil One and remain strong in your faith! Keeping the right perspective will help you come out of your wilderness season sooner.

In Deuteronomy 1:23 and 24, Moses sent out twelve spies to survey the land and take an inventory. Ten spies came back with a negative report, saying that the people in the land were stronger and taller than they were, the cities were large with walls reaching to the sky, and the Israelite people looked like grasshoppers compared to them. Why did they think that they looked like grasshoppers in their enemies' eyes? Quite simply, they did not have faith or the right perspective! They magnified the land's inhabitants over God. In other words, their focus shifted from faith to fear.

FEAR =
False
Evidence
Appearing
Real

An acronym for FEAR is **False Evidence Appearing Real.** They were seeing through the lenses of fear instead of faith. But the Scripture says that Joshua and Caleb returned with a positive report, saying they could surely take the land. In fact, the Scripture says that Caleb possessed a different spirit (Numbers 14:24). God's people have a different spirit because they carry the Spirit of God on the inside.

Therefore, God's people generally do not see like the world sees. Our faith is not in this world; rather, our faith is placed in the One who created it. As a result of their faith, Caleb and Joshua were the only two who would eventually enter the Promised Land because they chose to see the promise instead of the giants. They had God's perspective—not their own.

From Caleb and Joshua, we can learn that we must see things by faith—not from an earthly perspective. How are you seeing things while in your wilderness season? Are you seeing the promises of God or do you see your giants? Are you magnifying God, or do you magnify your giants? Your perspective in this season can either hinder your progression or help propel you forward. Is your perspective causing you to remain stuck—wandering in your wilderness? If so, immediately shift your focus off your giants and back onto the promises of God. When you feed one, the other will starve. By all means, feed your faith.

WHAT'S IN YOUR MOUTH?

While going through your wilderness season, keep the right attitude, the right perspective, and use the right words. A wilderness season is the time to keep a close guard over your mouth. The children of Israel wandered in the wilderness for forty years because of their murmuring and complaining. They had witnessed the hand of God watching over them and protecting them multiple times. They had seen how He had led them out of Egypt with a cloud by day and a pillar of fire by night. In spite of all they had witnessed, they allowed doubt and unbelief to enter their hearts and keep them from entering the Promised Land. Like the children of Israel, when you begin to complain, you will remain stuck and you will not progress forward in life. I like to say that complainers are "remainers."

Ever notice that people who complain are usually not going anywhere in life. They are miserable, so they complain, making everybody's life miserable as well. You've probably heard it said that misery loves company. How true! Miserable people like to bring others down with them. My advice to you if you want more out of life than where you are now, then stay away from complainers! Associate with people who are positive and who will encourage you to do better.

I have had the misfortune of being with people who complain. When they open their mouth to speak, I want to take off running because I know nothing good and uplifting will come forth. If you are not careful to guard your heart and your spirit against a complaining spirit, then you will be drawn in by it. Having a complaining spirit will cause you to wander around in the wilderness like the children of Israel with a lack of vision and purpose for your life.

I can remember when I went through a season of transition that did not transpire as I expected. After months of pressing in prayer and trying to push through all the discomfort from the stretching, I soon became discouraged. I started to take my eyes off Jesus and instead considering what I was going through. Frustration came when I couldn't break through all the opposition. Then I started to complain about not seeing any evidence of the promises that God had spoken to me. As a direct result of my complaining, my season of transition became worse because I started magnifying what I was going through instead of trusting God. I want to warn you, my friend, that complaining is a dangerous place to be with God. Basically, you are telling God that you don't trust Him.

The Old Testament contains an account of how the Israelites' complaining so angered God that He caused the ground to open up and swallow those who were murmuring and complaining. I realize that story is in the Old Testament, but the same principle still applies today. Complaining is a serious matter to God! To avoid bringing judgment on yourself, cease from complaining. Opening the door to a complaining spirit opens the door for other evil spirits.

A complaining spirit is like sticky glue; it attracts other spirits, draws you to it, keeps you stuck right where you are, and inhibits advancing or moving forward in the things of God. Complaining is a joy stealer and thrives on negativity, robbing the complainer of any joy in life. If you don't keep your focus on God, you will begin to always shift your focus on the negative side of matters. If you have been guilty of complaining, simply repent and get back on track with God. Watch your words!

What you speak either propels you forward or keeps you in bondage to the Enemy. *Death and life are in the power of the tongue, and those who love it will eat its fruit* (Proverbs 18:21 ESV). Are you speaking blessings or curses over yourself and your circumstance? Could it be the reason why you may not be seeing what you've been praying for is because of your spoken words? If you are speaking words of doubt and worry, then your words are giving life to the very things you are speaking. Because words are powerful, we can shift the atmosphere by what we are speaking. God demonstrated the power of words when He spoke the whole universe into existence. Are you being salt and light to those who do not know Christ—not only by your actions but also by your words? You must remember that your life is on display; you are being watched by those who do not know Jesus as their Savior.

The Bible says that we are ambassadors of Christ (2 Corinthians 5:20). According to the Merriam-Webster online dictionary, an *ambassador* is "an authorized representative or messenger."[1] Every believer is one of God's representatives and a messenger. The very words that a Christian says in conversations can either be a witness to others or water down his or her testimony. What kind of witness are you being with your words?

James 3:8b tells us that no human being can tame the tongue; *"It is a restless evil, full of deadly poison."* Watch what comes out of your mouth; once you release your words, you cannot retract them. Everyone will have to give an account on the Day of Judgment for every idle word spoken. By your words you will be acquitted, or by your words you will be condemned (Matthew 12:36-37). This Scripture should make us take our words into consideration before we release them. The very words that we speak can cause blessings to be released over our life *or* they can be a "blessing blocker" and cause our blessings to be withheld.

We can either help heal or hurt others with our words. Hurting others with our words is not demonstrating the love of Christ. I am sure we all can relate to times when someone spreads an untruth about us. The easiest way to retaliate is with hurtful words. But Romans 12:14 tells us to bless and not curse. When we were children, my mama would always say, "If you can't say anything nice, then don't say anything at all."

Yes, we all have missed the mark with our words, but when we know the truth of being held accountable for what we say, we can do better. *"For the flesh desires what is contrary to the Spirit, and the Spirit what is contrary to the flesh. They are in conflict with each other, so that you are not to do whatever you want"* (Galatians 5:17).

The apostle Paul said it like this:

> *"For I know that good itself does not dwell in me, that is, in my sinful nature. For I have the desire to do what is good, but I cannot carry it out. For I do not do the good I want to do, but the evil I do not want to do—this I keep on doing. Now if I do what I do not want to do, it is no longer I who do it, but it is sin living in me that does it"* (Romans 7:18-20).

Our flesh is in constant conflict with the spirit. What you feed will grow. If you starve your flesh, your spirit man will grow and become more sensitive to the things of God. You will be led by the Spirit—not by your flesh. If you are constantly feeding your flesh with negative talk and words, then you will see the fruit from it.

As children of God, we have to be careful of the words we speak; we cannot simply release anything we choose to speak because we know that the spiritual realms respond to words. You can speak things into existence with your words. If you are always making statements like, "I will always be single" or "I will always be broke—barely getting by," or "Things will always be this way" then, yes, you will have what you have because of what you are saying. You have given power to the negative things in your life. As a child of God, you have authority and power, so begin to decree and speak God's promises over your circumstance and you will begin to see His promises manifest in your life.

In the biblical account of Jesus' seeing the fig tree not bearing fruit in a season when it should have, He spoke to the tree saying, *"May no one ever eat fruit from you again"* (Mark 11:14a). The disciples heard Him, and when they returned, they saw the tree had withered and died (Mark 11:12-20). Jesus was demonstrating to His disciples the power of words.

When you are born again, the Holy Spirit comes and lives

on the inside of you. He will convict you of sin to the point that you cannot go on living the way you used to before you were saved. Not everyone understands this kind of language or commitment. But when you truly desire to be more like Jesus, getting rid of those things that are not like Him is a requirement. Of course, that decision includes watching our words.

The Enemy knows the power of words, and if he can persuade you to believe his lies and come into agreement with what he is saying, then you will begin to speak negatively either about your situation, yourself, or someone else. He knows if he can get you to believe his lies; you will soon begin to speak words of defeat over yourself and your circumstance—the very thing he desires to accomplish. Don't listen to Satan and his lies anymore! It's time to shut him up and put him under your feet where he belongs! James 4:7 says to submit to God, and *"Resist the devil, and he will flee from you."* How do we submit to God? Only by coming into agreement with His Word can we resist the Devil and his lies. By our standing on the Word of God, Satan must flee. The Devil cannot stand it when the Word of God is spoken at him. The Word of God is the most powerful weapon a Christian possesses.

Gossip is yet another snare—one of the easiest tactics the Enemy employs. In the third chapter of the book bearing his name, James tells us how hard it is to tame the tongue, even describing it is *"a restless evil, full of deadly poison"* (James 3:8 ESV).The lives of many people have been ruined and their character tarnished because of gossip and slander. God takes gossiping very seriously. Not only is gossip a sin, but Proverbs 11:13 states, *"A gossip betrays a confidence, but a trustworthy person keeps a secret."* When you know someone is a gossip, then you know that person is not trustworthy. My advice is to watch what information you share with a gossip because it won't stay between you two. When you are tempted to gossip, ask God to help to put a guard over your mouth and to help control your tongue.

FORGED IN THE FIRE

While going through your wilderness season, remember God is using this time to build a stronger foundation in Him. Trials and tribulations are used to build and strengthen us for what lies ahead. God refines us through the fiery trials of life. In the process of making pure gold, the goldsmith will put the gold in the fire and gradually turn up the heat so that all the impurities or the dross will rise to the surface. These impurities are skimmed off the surface of the molten gold. When the fire reaches 1,100 degrees Celsius, all of the impurities will surface, leaving behind pure gold. Isaiah 54:16a says, *"See, it is I who created the blacksmith who fans the coals into flame and forges a weapon fit for its work."* God's refining process is to put His child in the fire, testing him or her in the furnace of affliction to bring forth that child as pure gold. We never know what's on the inside of us until our faith is being tested.

> James 1:2-4, *"Consider it pure joy, my brothers and sisters, whenever you face trials of many kinds, because you know that the testing of your faith produces perseverance, Let perseverance finish its work so that you may be mature and complete, not lacking anything."*

Trials often come to reveal our true heart. When we are put under pressure, what is deep down in our hearts will begin to manifest and reveal what's truly on the inside. When the heat is applied, what's on the inside will surface to the top. Maybe you have been dealing with anger, and if that anger is not dealt with, it will surface when pressure is applied. God will use every trial to teach us lessons either about the trial that we are in, about ourselves, or will reveal something to us about Himself. Maybe before this trial, you never had a strong prayer life, but going through this trial has birthed a stronger prayer life in you. Maybe before this trial your faith was weak and you wavered during rocky times, but through this trial, God has taught you how to walk by faith and not by sight. Whatever the lesson maybe during this time, He knows what He is doing and what He is trying to accomplish in you.

As I have already mentioned, had God allowed to take the shorter route when they left Egypt, they would have been sorely defeated by the Philistines. They were not trained or ready to battle the Philistines. As we grow and mature in our faith, we also grow and mature in the battles that we face. A seasoned Christian can better handle the storms of life that a not-so-seasoned Christian isn't yet conditioned to handle. When I use the term "seasoned" Christian, I am describing a Christian who is mature in the faith and has stood firmly during the tests and trials of life. A non-seasoned Christian's faith may not be as strong and may waver or buckle under the pressure, but the seasoned Christian knows how to dig in his or her heels in a sort of speak and stand in faith.

YOU ARE COMING OUT

We all love seasons of rest, but seasons of war do come, and knowing the times and seasons we are in spiritually is important. Verses 1 and 8 of Ecclesiastes chapter 3 address *"a time for everything, and a season for every activity under the sun"* including *"a time for war and a time for peace."* If you willingly go into a battle that you are not authorized to engage in or prepared to fight on that spiritual level, then you can face some real danger spiritually. Taking this risk not only opens you up to some very heavy spiritual warfare but engaging in a spiritual battle without the Lord's consent or the leading of the Holy Spirit can be very dangerous. Not every battle that presents itself is meant for us to engage in, and having both discernment and wisdom in these matters will keep us from entering into unnecessary warfare. I am not saying to be passive about warfare but quite the opposite. We are in an aggressive spiritual battle daily; we have a very real Enemy who wants to take us out every single day. His number-one deception is to persuade every Christian to believe that he doesn't exist.

As every believer matures in his faith, he must be able to discern which battles he is to engage in as well as to have the wisdom to know which ones are not worth his time and energy. In other words, he must be careful not to waste his warfare on unnecessary battles.

When I became a new Christian, I thought I had to engage every spiritual battle that the Enemy threw my way. This ploy of the Enemy is to keep the Christian fighting insignificant battles so when a major battle arises, he is too worn out to fight. A seasoned warrior knows how to choose his battles wisely.

In 2 Timothy 2:4, the apostle Paul writes that no one serving as a soldier gets entangled in civilian affairs; rather, he tries to please his commanding officer. Your Enemy is spiritual, and his method of operation is quite strategic; he wants you to remain ignorant of his schemes and devices. But no Christian can remain ignorant of the Enemy's tactics; he is to be sober and alert.

The good news is that we have the greater One living within us. Our weapons of warfare are not carnal; they are mighty through God for demolishing and pulling down strongholds (2 Corinthians 10:4). *"For we wrestle not against flesh and blood..."* (Ephesians 6:12 KJV). We are in a spiritual war and, as Christians, we battle daily against Satan—not people; therefore, we must learn how to fight spiritually. Ephesians 6:10 tells us to put on the full armor of God in order to withstand the wiles of the Enemy.

One of my favorite sports is boxing. What makes a boxer great is not only his ability to throw a knockout punch but his stamina and endurance. A good boxer has to build up his stamina and endurance if wants to last in a match that continues beyond a few rounds. If he always manages to knock out his opponent in the first or second round, then he will never build up his lung capacity to endure a match beyond the first few rounds. Imagine the endurance required to be in a match lasting seven hours and nineteen minutes!

Our spiritual training can be likened to the training of a boxer. First, we have to get into spiritual shape and learn how to endure all types of situations meted out by the Enemy. These tactics of the Devil are used to help mature and strengthen us. Becoming a developed, mature fighter will require months of training. If God delivered His spiritual warrior from every battle in which he was engaged, he won't have the spiritual muscles to last a battle of months or years. God does not send His children trials and tribulations; rather, He uses them to help develop an unwavering faith and trust in Him. Standing firm on the Word of God will help sustain us during the storms and help build our faith.

In Matthew 7:24-27, Jesus talks about a person who puts His words into practice versus one who chooses not to put His words into practice. The person who puts these words into practice is like a wise man who builds his house on the rock. When the winds beat against the house and the rains flooded the streams, causing them to rise, the house did not fall because its foundation was on the rock. The one who chose not to listen is compared to a foolish man who built his house on sand. When the wind and rains came and the streams rose, that house fell with a great crash. I must admit when the storms came in my life, I wanted that trial to end quickly! Nobody likes enduring the storms of life—whether in the natural or spiritual aspect.

While living on the Gulf Coast, I learned how to endure or "ride out" storms. When a tropical storm or hurricane approaches, the news stations issue a warning to let the residents know about the impending storm. As the storm develops and becomes a potential threat or a danger, precautions must be taken such as issuing an evacuation plan or warning residents to seek shelter.

At times, life can be that way spiritually; we can see or sense things from afar and know that a potential spiritual storm is on the horizon, so to speak. We can begin to cover the situation in prayer. Sometimes, though, we may have little to no warning when a spiritual storm strikes, whether the sudden death of a loved one, a chronic illness, a relationship failure, or the loss of a job. If you are not deeply rooted in the Word of God, times like these can shake your foundation. Don't wait until a storm hits your life to start praying and reading the Word of God. Start today building a solid foundation in the Word—like the wise builder who was able to withstand the storm because his house was built on a firm foundation.

When times like these came in my life, if I had not known the Word of God that kept me anchored, I truly don't know if I would have survived. That's why, as a believer, we know the One who can see us through every battle and calm every raging storm in our life. His name is Jesus! Hallelujah!

Many generals of the faith, such as Moses and David, were trained in the wilderness before ever rising to greatness. David was trained in the wilderness by protecting his father's sheep from the roving lions and bears. Before he could possibly consider defeating Goliath, he had to kill a lion and a bear. I am sure you can look back over your life and see how God has trained and developed you spiritually.

I can testify that God has trained me to be a warrior in His kingdom. Of course, I did not get to this place overnight; I had to encounter certain circumstances to help mature and develop me to where I am now. And like you, we are all still being developed and fashioned daily. We are always in constant training, and we never stop learning.

We all have or will experience a wilderness season somewhere along our journey. When you are in a wilderness season, guarding your heart from any root of bitterness is so important. Before some go into their wilderness season, they start the journey on fire for God; however, sometimes enduring a long season in the wilderness opens the door to the Enemy's words of doubt and discouragement. If these people are not careful, they will begin to listen and believe the Enemy's lies. They begin to think that God has left them during this lengthy season.

My friend, as long as you keep the faith and the right perspective, you will come out of your wilderness season with more strength and faith in God. If you do find yourself in a dry season, may I encourage you not to despise this time? The Lord is giving you the opportunity to renew your spiritual life and remove hindrances from your life that may be keeping you from moving forward. Keep in mind that Jesus had to experience the wilderness too, but He used the Word of God to strengthen Him.

If you are in a wilderness season and you are feeling alone, God has not left you nor forgotten about you. I have had my share of wilderness seasons, and I wish I could testify of coming out of every one with the right perspective, but I didn't. I believe, for that reason, I can write about my experiences. In some of them, I came out strengthened; at other times, I came out battle-worn and weary because I failed to keep my focus on God. All I could think was *how much longer is this season going to last?* At times, I did not have the right attitude or perspective.

If this season has been difficult for you, ask God what He is trying to show you or teach you. Ask Him to strengthen your trust in Him and allow you to come out with an even stronger faith in Him than before. I promise you that this season won't last forever.

In Ezekiel chapter 37, God sends Ezekiel to a valley full of dry bones. As they were walking among the bones, God asked His prophet, *"Son of man, can these bones live?"* (Ezekiel 37:3a).

After examining the dry bones, Ezekiel replied, *"Sovereign* LORD, *you alone know"* (Ezekiel 37:3b). In other words, Ezekiel was saying, "In the natural, it doesn't look too good, but only You know, Lord."

God then told Ezekiel to prophesy to the dry bones. And as Ezekiel began to prophesy life over those dry bones they begin to come to life. *"There was a noise, a rattling sound, and the bones came together, bone to bone...and tendons and flesh appeared"* (Ezekiel 37:7b-8a).

Have you ever been in a seemingly hopeless situation in the natural? Maybe you've been battling an illness, and the doctors told you that the test results didn't look promising. Perhaps you and your spouse have been on the brink of divorce, and you are not sure if the relationship will last. But then God begins to speak to you, "Hey son or daughter, I know the situation looks bad to you right now, but I need you to trust Me. I want you to begin to prophesy and speak life into this situation, and as you do, I will begin to blow life back into what seemed hopeless." According to His promise, God will begin to move and resurrect what seemed lifeless or dead. You will begin to look back at what seemed dry and destitute that is now full of life and thriving.

Begin to prophesy the Word of the Lord over whatever area in your life may be like those dry bones. As you take God at His word, you will begin experience the *ruach*, which is the breath of God in that area. There will be an awakening to the things of God in your life again as well as a renewed zeal and freshness in your walk again.

In Psalm 23 David shares one of his wilderness experiences, describing it as *"the valley of the shadow of death."* Many theologians say this passage described what some call a "dark-night-of-the-soul" time for David. A *dark night of the soul,* can basically be described as "spiritual depression." Trust me, I am not implying that your wilderness experience will or should be like David's. Not only has David endured a night season, some of the greatest of Christians have suffered from this condition at one point in their journey of faith such as Jeremiah, the "Weeping Prophet," and Elijah.[2]

I can remember all too well going through a season of a "dark night of the soul." I had gone through a series of events in my life where I thought I would not make it through my season. Words fail me in trying to share the feelings of despair and loneliness that I was enduring. I felt as if I were holding on the Lord with everything that I had within me. Had it not been for certain people in my life like my parents and some of my closest friends who helped bring me out of my spiritual depression, I do not know where I might be today.

This experience was very uncomfortable because I am so used to hearing God's voice, but I felt that God was distant from me, leaving me alone to somehow navigate this season by myself. May I testify that you are not alone, and God has not left you? When I thought that He had abandoned me, He was teaching me to walk by faith—not by sight. Yes, I had to endure this uncomfortable, but also most powerful, season because I had to truly trust in Him when everything looked totally opposite. I was drawn closer to Him than ever before. I had to remember that His Word says that He will never leave me.

If you are walking in a "dark-night-of-the-soul" season, you will need to completely immerse yourself in His Word. You must recall and stand on all the promises that God spoke to you before you entered this season. Most importantly, guard your heart and mind. You cannot become focused on what the trial looks like in the natural because what you are experiencing is truly a faith walk. If you need help, of course you should reach out to others for help; don't suffer alone!

1 Ambassador," *Merriam-Webster.com,* https://www.merriam-webster.com/dictionary/ambassador, accessed 13 August 2019.

2 R. C. Sprouls, "The Dark Night of the Soul," *Tabletalk Magazine,* February 2018, https://tabletalkmagazine.com/?s=R+C+Sproul%2C+Dark+Night+of+the+Soul, accessed June 10, 2019.

Questions

1) If you've ever been through a wilderness season, what lessons has God taught you while going through this season?

2) What has the subtopic "What's in Your Mouth?" taught you? What really helped you? What stood out?

3) What have you learned about God while going through your wilderness season?

4) How has God used these lessons to help mold you and shape you more into His image?

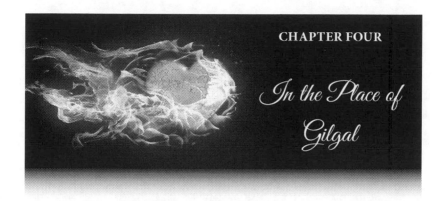

CHAPTER FOUR

In the Place of Gilgal

A Season of Transition

Then the LORD said to Joshua, "Today I have rolled away the reproach of Egypt from you." So the place has been called Gilgal to this day. – Joshua 5:9

FOR OVER FOUR hundred years, the Egyptians had held the children of Israel in slavery to the practices of their system and their gods. But God delivered them from the hand of their enemies and brought them out of their bondage to sin and slavery, rolling away the reproach of Egypt from them. According to the Merriam-Webster online dictionary, *reproach* means "an expression or rebuke or disapproval; to bring into discredit; or one who is subjected to scorn."[1]

Geographically, Gilgal is located on the eastern border of Jericho west of the Jordan River (Joshua 4:19). Gilgal is a place of transition, which symbolizes separating from the wilderness and being consecrated to God. An entire generation wandered in the wilderness for forty years, which allowed the disobedient older generation to die off (Numbers 32:13, Joshua 5:6). Despite the children of Israel's disobedience, God is a covenant-keeping God, and He still had plans for His people.

A new consecrated generation led by Joshua emerged out of the wilderness at Gilgal, ready to step into their destiny. But before the children of Israel were able to enter into the Promised Land, God told Joshua to circumcise the nation of Israel a second time (Joshua 5:2). All the men of military age who had left Egypt had now died in the wilderness, but all the people who were born in the wilderness during the journey from Egypt had not been circumcised (Joshua 5:4-5). Circumcision of the flesh was a sign of covenant between Abraham and God (Genesis 17:19-27).

After the men and boys were circumcised, they remained in Gilgal until they were healed (Joshua 5:8). The Israelites experienced a physical circumcision as an outward expression of their covenant to God. When we accept Jesus into our hearts, we experience a spiritual circumcision of the heart (Romans 2:28-29). Only through the blood of Jesus is the reproach of sin—your Egypt—rolled away from your life. You may be standing at your place of Gilgal and you have not fully entered into your Promised Land because the Lord may first require you to cut away or shed some things from your life.[2] There must be a necessary "cutting away" or *circumcision* of your flesh from the things of the world before you can step into what God has for you next.[3] You must remember that you are in the world, but not of the world. We are children of the Most High God, and we are not called to fit in with the world. We are called to be *peculiar* which means "different and set apart from the things of this world."[4]

What are the things of the world we must overcome that battle against our flesh? The Bible tells us the following in 1 John 2:15-16:

> *"Do not love the world or anything in the world.*
> *If anyone loves the world, love for the Father is*
> *not in them. For everything in the world—the lust*
> *of flesh, the lust of the eyes, and the pride of life—*
> *comes not from the Father but from the world."*

OUT WITH THE OLD, IN WITH THE NEW

When God brought the children of Israel out of Egypt, every time a problem arose, the people wanted to return to Egypt because that life was very familiar to them. In other words, they still possessed a wilderness mindset. Most of us will admit that embracing something new can be exciting, but scary at the same time—especially when it's unfamiliar to you. As you come into this new place with God, don't allow the fear of the unknown make you shrink back to where God brought you from. When things get tough and darkness looms, you'll begin to doubt and question God and want to return to what you knew before. I want to encourage you to keep moving forward and to resist the urge to turn back.

Gilgal was a place of healing.[5] God will begin to perform a healing work within you so that He can bring you into what He has promised you. As God begins to deal with your flesh, Gilgal can become a place of nakedness and vulnerability.[6]

After Joshua circumcised the Israelite men and they were healing, they experienced a time of nakedness and vulnerability. If their enemy living in nearby Jericho had known about their state of vulnerability, they could have taken advantage of them.[7] The Israelites had no other choice but to trust God with their safety.

We have all been in a place of vulnerability and nakedness at one time or another. Though scary and uncomfortable, a state of vulnerability strips away our pride and self-control, which is exactly where God wants us. We all struggle with being vulnerable because we want acceptance from others, but we don't need anyone to accept us. We are already loved and accepted by the One who created us and who knows every detail of our life. His is the only acceptance for whom you should live.

Before He can bring you into your Promised Land, you must stop and heal from your past—like the children of Israel did.[8] You must also confront your past so that you can step into your new directive. You cannot take your past into the new life that God is giving you. Don't allow the Enemy to push you backward into your past. The shame and reproach of your past sins were rolled away when you accepted Jesus into your heart as your Savior. The truth is, we all have a past but don't allow your past to determine your future. Your past is exactly that—your past.

Your past does not define who you are now; you are a new creature in Christ. The old you is no more. God's mercies are new every morning, and He showers you with His mercy and grace. Every day that you have breath, you have been given another opportunity by our Heavenly Father.

One of my favorite Scriptures is Philippians 3:13, which says, *"I do not consider myself yet to have taken hold of it. But one thing I do: forgetting what is behind and straining toward what is ahead."* What God has for you is ahead of you—not behind you. You have no need to stay there and continue to replay in your mind the things from your past because you cannot change anything; you cannot add a single hour to your life (Matthew 6:27). If you have repented of your sins and are born again, then God does not remember your sins anymore. In fact, Psalm 103:12 says they are removed—*"as far as the east is from the west."*

The blood of Jesus is far more powerful than your sins, your past mistakes, and even your current upset in which you may find yourself right now. No pit is too deep that God cannot rescue you out of it. The time has come to leave the old behind so that God can bring you into what He now wants for your life. *"Forget the former things; do not dwell on the past, see I am doing a new thing!"* (Isaiah 43:18-19a). Before God does that "new thing" in your life, you must take off the old self, which is your old way of thinking. How can you embrace the new with the same old mindset? It's time to remove the old wineskin. You cannot pour new wine into old wineskins for the old wineskins cannot contain the new wine and will burst (Mark 2:22).

God has prepared some things for you that will require your having a renewed mind for you to be able to grab a hold of what's getting ready to take place in your life. You cannot afford to continue thinking or feeling as you once did. Begin to declare daily over yourself that you have the mind of Christ. Practice taking every thought captive and guard your mind and heart. Move forward into the things of God. No more sitting in that place of lack and defeat!

The place that God is about to bring you into is a place of abundance and favor. The place where you are striving will cease, and you will begin to experience His divine rest. In this place God will begin to defy your enemies as He prepares a table for you in their presence. You are now standing at the door, getting ready to cross over into the land of your promise. You are being prepared as you wait patiently in the narrow hallway of your destiny. As you wait in that in-between place, continue to praise Him.

In the Waiting

In today's fast-paced society, no one likes to wait—whether in the grocery store, a drive-thru, in traffic, or in a doctor's office. We all tend to become impatient when it comes to waiting, but the waiting is what produces in us the fruit of the Spirit. When we are not willing to wait on God, we can get ahead of Him and cause a disaster, thereby hindering what God has in store for us. Yes, God's sovereign and compassionate nature still does not disregard the consequences of our actions.

Many of the people in the Bible experienced seasons of waiting. Abraham and Sarah waited on Isaac, their promised heir, for years before seeing the promise manifest. After years of being unable to conceive, Sarah grew weary in the wait and sought a way to help fulfill God's promise to Abraham. She offered Hagar, her Egyptian bondservant, in marriage to Abraham to bear him a child (Genesis 16:1-4). She soon discovered that her plan created a disaster—not only in her life, but also in the life of her promised son Isaac. When Isaac grew older, Ishmael began to mock his half-brother, so Sarah ordered Abraham to send away Hagar and Ishmael. None of these events would have transpired if she had only waited patiently on the

———

promise that had spoken to them instead of taking matters into her own hands.

Ishmael was birthed out of the flesh—not from the promise. Even though Ishmael would not be a part of the Abrahamic Covenant, God did promise that He would also increase Ishmael's descendants and make him numerous, but he would not be an heir to the promise—only Isaac. The Scripture says, *"Abraham had two sons, one by the slave woman and the other by the free woman. ²³His son by the slave woman was born according to the flesh, but his son by the free woman was born as the result of a divine promise"* (Galatians 4:22-23).

Yes, I can say that I understand where you are and how frustrating and discouraging waiting can be, especially when you are so close to stepping into what God has spoken to you. But don't lose hope in your waiting. Isaiah 40:31 (KJV) promises that *"They that wait upon the LORD shall renew their strength; they shall mount up with wings as eagles; they shall run, and not be weary; they shall walk, and not faint."* While you are patiently waiting, God will renew your strength as you continue to trust Him.

However, if you are not willing to wait on God and you begin to take matters into your own hands, thinking that you know better than God for your life, trust me, friend, you are making a huge mistake! You will end up further delaying what God has in store for you. We all want to take control and fix things when we feel things are not happening fast enough, but you do not want to birth something from the flesh that will be void of having God's anointing on it. Trust me, you want His anointing on what you are birthing because His anointing makes all the difference. I wouldn't want to risk doing anything that does not have God's anointing.

Let me say this, friend, God is not slack concerning His promises to you. He desires to give you all that He has promised to you, but His promises will be fulfilled in His timing—not yours. God is showing you how much He loves you by not bringing you into the fulfillment of the promise before you are ready. The Enemy wants you to think that God has forgotten about you, but God knows that if He gives you everything that He has promised when you think you should have it, then you won't be able to handle it. If you are not yet mature enough, fulfilling His promises can have the potential of destroying your life or your relationship with Him. Therefore, do not run ahead of God; wait for His time. Though God created time, He is not confined by it; He knows exactly when the time is best for you.

If you find yourself in a waiting season, don't become discouraged or impatient. While you are waiting, you are preparing for your harvest and the fulfillment of the promise that God spoke to you. Perhaps you are waiting for a prodigal child to return home, or maybe you are trusting Him for the salvation of a loved one, or perhaps you are single and have been waiting for a spouse—in whatever the situation, trust God and His timing. Many confuse waiting with being passive, but a waiting period is not the time to be passive; rather, it is a time of preparation.

Preparation always precedes promotion. Before Joseph was promoted to the palace, he was first being prepared in the pit. Before Esther was crowned queen, she had to go through months of a beautification preparation. Before David rose to greatness, he had to be prepared and trained in the wilderness while tending his father's sheep. The point is, if you are fretting because it seems you've been in your waiting season too long, I want to remind you that you're in good company! You are right where you should be. None of the examples I shared rose to their level of influence overnight; they had to endure seasons of waiting. As God's servant, faithfulness in the small matters prepares us for greater things in His kingdom.[9] You cannot see the potential of an oak tree in its seed form, but within that seed lies the potential of the oak tree's greatness. Therefore, do not despise your day of small beginnings (Zechariah 4:10). Your season of waiting is not in vain; God is preparing you for what lies ahead of your destiny.

What is most important to understand is what God is teaching you in your season of waiting. Often, you will see things begin to manifest in you that you need to address. For example, in what area(s) pertaining to the fruit of the Spirit is your attention needed? Most of all, you want to avoid taking matters into your own hands and ultimately creating a disaster. Just choose to trust God.

In all honesty, waiting on what God has promised has been a true test of patience for me. I haven't always worn a smile on my face, and the waiting hasn't always been pretty. Yes, I have battled loneliness for years with nights of tears, but I would far rather wait on God's perfect timing than try to address matters on my own and make my life a disaster.

THE DEVOTED THINGS

Another reason why the previous generation could not settle in the Promised Land was because of idolatry. The Lord had commanded them not to make any idol or worship them (Exodus 20:4). However, after hundreds of years of being held in slavery to the Egyptians, the children of Israel disobeyed God and conformed to the Egyptian way of culture and began to worship their gods. I recall the story in Joshua chapter 7 of how the Israelite army went out to battle against their enemy, the Amorites, and was soundly defeated. Joshua discovered the defeat happened because of sin in their camp. Achan, who was from the tribe of Judah, had violated God's command and had stolen some of the plunder from Jericho that had been consecrated to God. He had then hidden them in the ground under his tent. His part in taking these "devoted things" involved the entire nation as the Israelites had been commanded not to take any possessions for themselves. However; due to Achan's sin, thirty-six men in the Israelite army were struck down and defeated by their enemy.

You cannot go forward into your Promised Land until you have rid yourself from any "devoted things" or idols that may be hidden in your heart. You may be saying, "I don't have any idols in my life." But idols of the heart, be it a person, a place, or a thing, can be subtle. If you have someone or something in your life that you place before God, then that person or thing is an idol. According to Matthew 10:37, your family can be an idol. *"Anyone who loves their father or mother more than me is not worthy of me; anyone who loves their son or daughter more than me is not worthy of me."* Your job, money, worldly possessions, and now, most Christian's idols involve social media. I am shocked at the amount of time most Christians spend on social media rather than in the Word of God. Then we wonder why our life is not where it should be. Let's start with where we are spending most of our time. I have been guilty of spending too much time on other interests, but now I monitor how much time I spend on social media versus being in the Word of God. I have become far more aware of how the Enemy can be so subtle in our lives.

What areas are you more devoted or committed to than

your relationship with God? Is this interest hindering you from moving forward in your Christian life? Check your heart, pray, and ask God to show you if you have any "devoted things" that you have placed before Him in your life. When God reveals an area to you, repent and ask Him to remove whatever it is from your heart. God should always be first priority in your life.

God told Joshua until they removed the devoted things from among them, they could not stand against their enemies (Joshua 7:13). My friend, God wants us to get rid of anything in our heart that we have in common with the Enemy—whether its anger, a lack of forgiveness, fear—whatever it may be. You will not have victory over your enemies until you first remove anything in your heart that has become an idol. You may have been walking with Jesus for years, but you could still have areas in your heart that have not been fully surrendered to Him. Full freedom doesn't happen in your life all at once; that freedom comes in seasons of layers in your walk. If you have anything that may have taken God's place in any area, then you may be giving the Enemy an open door of access to your life. You won't experience the fullness of Christ until you have completely surrendered every area of your life to Him.

God knows what areas need work and how they are holding you back from experiencing His fullness. He is the Master Gardener who knows what needs to be pruned in your life to make you even more fruitful. John 15:1-2 says, *"I am the true vine, and my Father is the gardener. ²He cuts off every branch in me that bears no fruit, while every branch that does bear fruit he prunes so that it will be even more fruitful."* God does not prune the areas that are dead; He cuts them off. He prunes the areas that are alive and fruitful so that you will bear even more fruit, showing yourselves to be His disciples.

My mother loves her garden, and at times, I would watch how she would prune her rose bushes. At times I would think, *will there be anything left on this tree?* What she was doing was getting the tree ready for its next season by cutting away the dead areas on the rose bushes that would hinder their growth. When the season came, the bushes grew bigger and produced even more roses than the previous season. In the same way, when God prunes His children, we don't necessarily enjoy His snipping. The snips can be painful but necessary for our spiritual growth. He has to remove anything in our life that hinders our spiritual walk. Bearing fruit means becoming more like Jesus, and without the pruning process, we will remain unfruitful in our walk.

Gilgal is the place where the wrestling with yourself and with God comes to an end as you completely surrender to the Lord and to the work He wants to do in your life. Have you ever wrestled with God over some matter? I am sure we all can agree with having wrestled with God at some time in our Christian walk. Jacob, who would be renamed Israel, wrestled with an angel of the

Lord until daybreak. During his lengthy struggle, he went from struggle to success. The area of your greatest struggle can become the area of your greatest victory. Refuse to give up and quit.

Gilgal is also a place of remembrance.[10] At Gilgal, Joshua set up twelve stones that had been taken out of the Jordan River as a monument of God's faithfulness and how they had crossed the river on dry ground (Joshua 4:20-21). I feel sure that you can look back over your life, and you may not have to look very far to witness times of God's faithfulness. Leaving behind a legacy as a testimony to your children of God's faithfulness is important. Therefore, never fail to share your testimony with others of God's faithfulness. I can definitely say that my life is a testimony to others and especially to my son about the faithfulness of God. I can look back and remember all that the Lord has brought us through and still continues to do so.

Looking back in awe and with gratitude will remind you of God's faithfulness and how He has delivered you from your trials. These moments of reflection help strengthen you and build your faith when facing trying times. Before David defeated Goliath, he remembered how God had delivered him from the lion and from the bear. He recalled God's faithfulness to deliver him during his time of trouble. The Lord who delivered you then can surely deliver you now.

Gilgal is a place of divine provision. Along their journey in the wilderness, God miraculously provided manna for the children of Israel, and when they grew tired of eating manna, they begged for meat. God provided them with quail. When they came to Gilgal, they celebrated the Passover; the day after, they ate some of the produce of the land. The manna stopped appearing the day after they ate this food from the Promised Land; that year and from then on, they ate the produce of Canaan (Joshua 5:10-12).

We often say where God guides, He also provides; I have found this statement to be true. Where God is leading you, He will provide for you. As God supernaturally provided manna in the wilderness, He can also provide for you. You don't have to worry about how or if His plan will work; you merely have to obey God and trust His leading. God is the Supplier, and He will supply all your needs (Philippians 4:19). Manna, which was the Israelites' food in the wilderness, stopped and the people ate from the produce of Canaan which represented abundance and blessing.

You may be in a place of transition and now that God has done a healing work in your heart, you will now experience the overflow of His promises. A transformation of newness awaits you as you prepare your heart. You will no longer be wandering around in circles season after season. With the conclusion of your dry season, you can sense the zeal that you once embraced before you entered your long, dry wilderness season. The fire that you once had in your walk with Christ will be reignited in your heart. You are now ready to cross into your Promised Land.

Questions

1) What are or have been some area(s) in your past which have resulted in having difficulty in moving forward?

2) What has your waiting season taught you? Can you identify any area(s) on which you need to work while you are waiting?

3) To what area(s) in your life have been more devoted than to God? (These areas could be anything such as family, friends, hobbies, your job or even social media.)

---

1   "Reproach," *Merriam-Webster.com*, https://www.merriam-webster.com/dictionary/reproach, accessed 13 August 2019.

2   David Landry, "Memorial Stones and Covenant Reminders: Joshua 4:1-5:12," *Calvary Chapel of Casa Grande, AZ*, May 15, 2015, https://networkcmo.com/_content/ userdata/67/.../Joshua41to5125784175b45272.pdf.

3   *Ibid.*

4   "Peculiar," *Merriam-Webster.com*, https://www.merriam-webster.com/dictionary/peculiar, accessed 13 August 2019.

5   E. Keith Hassell, "Come, let us go to Gilgal," *Faith- life Sermons.com*, 2005, https://sermons.fathlife.com/ sermons/20185-come-let-us-go-to-gilgal.

6   Benjamin Khoo, "Gilgal before Jericho," *Prophetic Insights for His Glory*, March 9, 2011, https://priestly- bride.blogspot.com/2011/03/gilgal-before-jericho.html.

7   *Ibid.*

8   David M. Colburn, "Joshua 1-24 (Taking the Promised Land)," *Bible.org*, August 2012, https://bible. org/seriespage/23-joshua-1-%E2%80%93-24-taking- promised-land.

9   Dr. David Jeremiah, *The Jeremiah Study Bible, NKJV: What It Says. What It Means. What It Means for You,* Franklin, Tenn.: Worthy Publishing, 2013.

10   Gerald Van Horn, "The Memorial of Victory," *Sermon Central,* January 24, 2006, www.sermonscentral. com/sermons/the-memorial-of-victory-gerald-van- horn-sermon-on-christian-discplines-87689.

CHAPTER FIVE

Do You Want to Get Well?

Here is a great number of disabled people used to lie—the blind, the lame, and the paralyzed. ⁵One who was there had been an invalid for thirty-eight years. ⁶When Jesus saw him lying there and learned that he had been in this condition for a long time, he asked him, "Do you want to get well?"

⁷"Sir," the invalid replied, "I have no one to help me into the pool when the water is stirred, while I am trying to get in, someone goes down ahead of me." ⁸Then Jesus said to him, "Get up! Pick up your mat and walk." ⁹At once the man was cured; he picked up his mat and walked.... – John 5:3-9

WHEN I FIRST read this account, my first thought was, *why in the world did Jesus ask someone in this condition a question like "Do you want to get well"?* His question seems somewhat insensitive to someone who has been in this condition for a lengthy time, but Jesus never asks us a question for His own benefit, but for ours. The Scripture account says the man had been afflicted for thirty-eight years. An angel of the Lord would come at a certain time of the year to stir the waters and whoever was first to step into the waters after it had been stirred was healed of whatever disease he or she had. Because of his affliction, he had missed his opportunity to be healed thirty-eight times.

My question is: did he really want to be healed? Did he truly desire deliverance from this condition?

If you were in such a situation for such a lengthy time and you were desperate for your breakthrough, would you let anything stand in the way of your getting your healing and deliverance? True deliverance requires humility and vulnerability to the point that you don't care what it takes or what others may say or think about you. You must come to the end of yourself and do whatever it takes to be delivered. If you care more about your image and reputation, then you are not ready for deliverance. Real deliverance can be messy with no room for pride when you truly want deliverance. Pride will hinder a person from being fully delivered.

The woman who had the issue of blood for twelve years was so desperate for her healing that she pressed her way through the crowd to get to Jesus. She had exhausted all her options in the natural, and she said within herself, "If I could only touch the hem of His garment, I would be healed." That is faith, my friend! She pressed her way through every opposition standing in the way of her healing.

In the Old Testament, someone who had a bleeding condition was considered unclean; therefore, you can imagine the scorn, humiliation, and rejection that she likely endured. The label that had been placed on her as a result of this infirmity most likely kept her isolated from her family, friends and community. Still, she pressed her way through the crowd and their "labels" in order to receive her miracle. She did not miss her opportunity when it was presented.

We must make sure that when certain opportunities present themselves, we are ready and in position to take them because we never know when we may be given another chance. Mark chapter 10 includes the story about a blind man named Bartimaeus who sat begging by the roadside. When he heard that Jesus was passing by, he began to shout. When people began to rebuke him and telling him to be quiet, he shouted even louder.

May I say at this point that your shout will always irritate folks who do not understand where you've been, what you had to go through to get where you are now, and how long you've waited for your breakthrough. Glory! That's a message all by itself!

What if he had kept quiet when others told him to be quiet?

What if he had allowed pride or fear of what others said get in the way of his receiving his miracle? He would have missed his opportunity of healing when it was presented to him. Don't allow people to box you in and make you conform to their ways because they lack faith to believe for themselves. If you allow them, people will project their fears and lack of unbelief onto you. If you are desperate for God, then good! Desperate people are hungry people, and hungry people always get God's attention. When you become desperate enough for change, you will let go of all the excuses.

The Scripture mentions that a great number of disabled people, including the blind, the lame, and the paralyzed stayed near this pool. This man who was healed after 38 years was identified as being among this group of people. Like people attract their own kind. We can remain in a situation for so long that we no longer desire growth or change, and we begin to live a mediocre lifestyle. We start to become complacent with our surroundings and soon stop believing that life can change for us. Who surrounds us can have an effect on our perspective—either in a positive or a negative way. If we are surrounded by people who are not aspiring to have a better lifestyle and continue to remain in the same place of lacking year after year, then we can begin to adapt and pattern our life after them. In other words, we will become a product of our environment.

My parents, especially my father, were very careful of our

associations when we were growing up because he knew the power of influence. He did not tolerate our being around people who would have a bad influence on us. I Corinthians 15:33b says, *"Bad company corrupts good character."* Those who surround us can affect our lives for good or bad. We can start to lose hope and begin to doubt that things would change for us and that our lives would ever get better. This loss of hope is not of God; this doubt comes straight from the Enemy, who wants you to give up and stop pursuing what God has for you. Of course, the Enemy wants you to remain in that same situation —neither advancing nor moving forward into the things of God.

God's kingdom, which is not stagnant, is always advancing and moving forward. In order for the child of God to move forward, he must divorce himself from the lies of Satan and choose to believe what God's Word says about him and his future. Trust me, God always has more for His children.

I believe if the lame man had really desired healing, then no one would have beat him to the pool. At some point, one of his attempts would have been successful. I can understand his being unable to get into the pool the first few times, but not thirty-eight times! At some point, he should have come up with a plan of action and what steps needed to be taken in order to be the first person to reach the pool.

According to Scripture, he had one chance to be healed every year, but he kept missing it repeatedly. Sometimes we can become so focused on other people that we miss divine moments and opportunities when they are presented to us.

What divine moments and opportunities have you missed because you have allowed excuses to stop you from moving forward? What are some steps that you can take in your life for the better? Friend, it's time to let go of all the excuses. As you begin to trust God and move forward, God will honor your obedience. Our faith should not be placed in people because even those with good intentions fail us at times. We fail others simply because we are flawed and imperfect beings; however, our faith should be placed in God alone who remains faithful and never wavers even when we are not faithful.

If we are not careful, looking for people to help us when we should be looking to God can develop into a co-dependence on that person. No, I am not saying don't ever allow anyone to help you, but don't simply sit around, waiting for others to help make your situation better when God has already given you the tools for what you need to come out of your situation.

Jesus gave the lame man a solution to his problem. He commanded, "Get up! Pick up your mat and walk." His first instruction to this man was to simply start moving! In other words, this man with an infirmity had to participate in his own deliverance. He had to get up from the place with which he had become so familiar. Obeying Jesus required faith and action on his part—not someone else's. He couldn't depend on someone else; he had to be willing to put in the work for himself. Just like the man who laid there on his mat, you can't simply sit waiting for change to come to you. If you truly desire change, you must put in the work to see that change take place.

What has become your "mat," so to speak? To what have you been holding that has kept you stagnant and robbed you of your freedom in Christ? What have you allowed to become a crutch in your life? If you have been holding onto pain, unforgiveness, or rejection, the time has come for you to get up from that place, pick up your "mat," and walk into everything that God has for you. Don't stay there; God has given you a way of escape. No more waiting! Your freedom is now available for you in Christ.

WHAT ARE YOU WAITING FOR? MOVE!

Deuteronomy 1:6 through 8 shares how the Lord told Moses at Horeb that the children of Israel had stayed long enough at that mountain, and the time had come for them to break camp, advance, and take possession of the land that He had given them. God told them to go in and take possession of the land that He had promised them; instead, they had become complacent with wandering right where they were.

What dream or desire has God placed inside of you? Have you settled for less than what God has promised you? Maybe you had a dream of opening your own business, but instead you have settled for the job you have now. If you want to see change, you must be willing to do something different than what you have been doing.

My friend, be willing to take the first step toward your dream! That step may look like stepping out to seek a business license. Maybe you desire to be healthy this year. If so, step out by signing up at a gym, committing to eating healthier, and sticking to a workout routine. I cannot know what changes you need to make…just don't be content with your current level or status. God has more for you than where you are now. I don't know about you, but I want all that God has for me. I refuse to settle for an average or mediocre lifestyle when I know He has more for me. Trust me, the same promises are available for you. God says you are the head and not the tail—above and not beneath (Deuteronomy 28:13). Declare and speak His promises over yourself.

Part of my testimony of being a single parent is that my son and I lived in low-income housing and on government assistance for years. I desperately wanted change for both of us. I knew this was not the life that Jesus had promised me. I reached the point where I became very frustrated. I had done everything I knew to do, including putting myself through school and working at the same time. Year after year, I seemed to remain stuck—surrounded by others who were in a situation similar to mine. In no way am I belittling anyone who has to stay in low-income housing or has to be temporarily on government assistance in order to help care for their family.

Trust me, I know what it's like to stand in a welfare line, but poverty is not my portion, and neither is it yours. I am saying that if I wanted change to take place in my life, I had to do my part for change to take place. I evaluated my current situation and made the necessary changes in my life for what I wanted to see take place. I had to be intentional about making some adjustments that required my stepping out and trusting God—even when it looked like the opposite of what I was seeing in the natural. Remember, faith is an action word; it's not based on what we can see in the natural. Faith comes by hearing and hearing by the word of God (Romans 10:17).

If you desire change, you must be willing to position yourself for it. Your willingness is the key that will unlock change in your life. You cannot simply sit and wait for things to come to you. Change takes effort on your part—not someone else's. For thirty-eight years, this man did not try to position or prepare himself for the change that he so desired. Preparation comes with taking the necessary steps in order to shift your life in that direction. He was so concerned with someone's helping him get into the waters that he missed his opportunity year after year.

As a matter of fact, his response to the question when Jesus asked him if he wanted to get well was that he had no one to help him get into the waters when they were being stirred. He did not respond with a simple "yes" to the question; instead, he gave an excuse for his failure. In other words, what he was really saying was, "The reason why I am not healed is because I have no one to help me get healed." We must be careful not to place blame on others; rather, we must be willing to take responsibility for our own mistake and be willing to admit why we are not seeing the results that we desire in our own life.

The real issue wasn't that he couldn't get into the water; the real reason was his lack of faith. He stopped believing for change in his life, so instead he expected someone to help him. We cannot place all our hope and trust in other people to the point of putting our hopes and dreams on hold. Yes, I understand that we need people in life and that we are not meant to walk our journey alone, but we cannot become so dependent on others that we allow what others can or cannot do for us stop us from pursuing our dreams. When something has to be done, I have always been the kind of person who doesn't procrastinate; I get the job done. I am a no-nonsense kind of person.

Sometimes we can allow what we are going through to begin to dim our hopes and expectations that our life can change for the better—especially if we've been in that situation for an extended amount of time. The Scripture says in Proverbs 13:12a, *"Hope deferred makes the heart sick,"* which means that allowing hopelessness to come into your heart will snuff out your dreams and desires. Friend, please don't allow the Enemy to push you into a hopeless state of thinking that things will never change for you.

If we are not careful, our pain can become a crutch in our life. If that is the case in your life, you will start to become comfortable in our own dysfunction. Some people will remain comfortable with you as long as you remain in your dysfunctional state; however, your beginning to grow and coming out of your dysfunction threatens their comfort level. They feel uncomfortable because your growth challenges them to make some changes in their own life. Growth is always intimidating to those who don't like change. So, keep growing!

YOU ARE THAT MAN!

In 2 Samuel chapter 12, the Lord sent Nathan the prophet to confront David about his sin. In chapter 11 when a king normally went off to war with his soldiers, David stayed behind (v.1). One evening while he was walking on the roof of the palace, he noticed Bathsheba bathing and sent for her (vv. 2-4). The affair led to a pregnancy, and in an attempt to cover his sin, he sent Uriah, Bathsheba's husband, to the frontlines of battle to be killed. God then sends the prophet Nathan to confront David about his sin.

Nathan tells David an allegory about a traveler with one lamb who came to a rich man and how the rich man refrained from selecting his own sheep or cattle to prepare a meal. Instead, the rich man selected the lamb that belonged to the poor man to prepare a meal (2 Samuel 12:4). Upon hearing this story, David became incensed and wanted the rich man to pay for what he'd done to the poor man.

Then Nathan said to David, "You are the man!" (2 Samuel 12:7a). David already knew that what he had done was wrong, yet he tried to make his sin right by attempting to hide it.

Let's get this straight: nothing—absolutely nothing—can be hidden before God. You cannot cover up your sin and pretend that God does not see or know about it because He does. He sees and knows all things. Yes, God is loving, and He forgives us when we mess up, but that forgiveness does not exempt us from the consequences of our sin. God is good in that He lovingly disciplines and corrects His children when they are wrong; He chastises those He loves. If He didn't love us, He wouldn't discipline us when we get off track. None of His children enjoy the discipline part of His love, which is only for our good. No parent enjoys disciplining his or her children, but every parent knows discipline is for the good of the child.

Despite David's being king and a man after God's own heart, he was still a flawed man like us, and he was not exempt from the consequences of his actions; no one is. What ultimately happens in our lives represents the consequences of our actions. We cannot choose what the consequences from our actions will be.

At times, we can be like David—so quick to want an injustice addressed that we fail to realize our own sin. For that reason, self-examination is so important. Maybe we hear about an injustice done to a family member or a close friend, and in our desire for justice on their behalf, we forget about praying for God to show that person mercy and to come to repentance. We serve a loving God who will forgive when we ask, but we should also do likewise in forgiving others when they sin against us or against someone we love. *"Love covers over a multitude of sins"* (I Peter 4:8).

The story of David and Bathsheba is not one of condemnation. Their story of conviction and correction teaches us to look within ourselves and ask God to show us if we have failed to see our own shortcomings. God forbid that we go on in life thinking that we are right with God when we are trying to cover up the sin that may be in our life. If you are having trouble with sin—whatever it may be—don't try to cover it up; bring it before God and ask Him to help you. We all fall at times, but don't stay there. Get back up and continue your race! God won't leave you helpless, but He will help you in your weaknesses. By all means, do not walk around being so sin-focused and legalistic that you forget about God's grace. His grace is sufficient when we miss the mark but is not a license to continue sinning.

When Nathan knew about David's sin, he did not expose David publicly. He did not go around gossiping and telling others about what David had done. Nathan addressed David's sin in confidence. I am sure we all know what it feels like to share sensitive information with someone, and that person does not hold the information in confidence. That breach of trust hurts you to the core. Nathan evidently had a close relationship with David, and therefore, he had access to speak into David's life. Correction can be received when we have a relationship with the person who has sinned. Correcting someone with whom you do not have a genuine relationship will come across as being critical and judgmental. More than likely, that person will not receive the correction—even though it may be the truth. That's why it's so important to build relationships with people we can trust and who will hold us accountable when we are weak in certain areas.

I know you've heard stories of famous entertainers whose lives took a turn for the worse, and they ended up nearly destroying their lives all because they were surrounded by people who continually said yes to them and their desires, endorsing their wrong behavior. They received no accountability from those surrounding them. They had no one to speak truth into their life and encourage them to do right. No one told them "no" or that they were headed down the wrong path. Being surrounded by "yes men" in your life might not be very wise; having people who will love you enough to tell you like it is shows wisdom. I call those who speak truth "straight shooters."

I feel fortunate to have a few straight shooters in my life, and I honor and respect them for who they are because they speak from a place of love—not condemnation. They truly want and desire what's best for my life. If you are surrounded by friends who go along with everything you say or do even if some of those things are not healthy, then the time has come to evaluate your circle of friends. Surround yourself with people who will hold you accountable to doing right.

No Grit, No Glory

I feel relatively sure you've probably heard the idiom, "No grit, no glory," which can be summed up as having the courage to overcome. *Grit* is defined in the *Merriam-Webster Online Dictionary* as "courage and resolve, strength of character."[1] In reading about the formation of a pearl, I discovered that the jewel begins as a mere irritant that gets inside an oyster's shell. The oyster secretes a substance that coats the irritant in layers until a pearl is formed. What started out as agitation and showed no significance or substance to the oyster became something of great value.

We may go through some issues in life that seem insignificant at the time, but the truth is, even the minor, seemingly insignificant issues of life are meant to help others overcome. We are to share the experiences that we've endured in order to help others. When you go through a crisis or a trial in life, you can empathize with others when they are experiencing something similar. You know what it feels like to go through that situation; therefore, you can help others because you have been through the same test of life. Testing will birth compassion in our hearts for those who are hurting.

Compassion is one of the many attributes of God. Matthew 9:36 says that Jesus was moved with *compassion*, which is "the ability to empathize with one's pain and suffering."[2] The compassion of God creates an inward desire in us to see others healed, delivered, and set free. When you have been there yourself, you can empathize with others who are hurting and suffering. You cannot heal what you don't feel. When we go through a personal trial or through suffering and come out of it victorious because of God's grace, we are able to empathize and feel the hurt and pain of others because we have experienced that same situation.

If you have never been in poverty, then how can you minister to someone who is? If you have never been bound and oppressed, then how can you minister to someone who needs deliverance? What you have already overcome, you can witness to others who are going through the same situation. A different level of depth and weight is placed on someone who has gone through the fire of that trial versus someone who has not. You can sense the raw pain and weight, as well as hear the life and healing in the words of a person who has been there.

God brought you out so that you can be a deliverer to others who are in bondage. No pain or trial is ever wasted in our lives; Jesus uses it all. He causes all things to work for our good (Romans 8:28).

All throughout the New Testament, we read stories of Jesus' healing those who were sick, oppressed, and broken. John 4:1-42 tells the story about the Samaritan woman. Despite the cultural differences that separated the Jews and Samaritans from associating with each other, Jesus went to Samaria. He had an appointment with a broken woman at a well, a woman who needed a revelation about the true Living God. Jesus engaged in a conversation with her by asking her one simple question: "Will you give Me a drink?" Her willingness to fulfill His request allowed Jesus to tell her who He is—the Living Water, and for her to open up about her life. Jesus was able to lovingly confront her about her life and the sin in which she was involved. One conversation opened the door for this woman to accept salvation.

As a result of her salvation, she returned to her hometown to share her testimony, and many were saved (John 4:39). Talk about Evangelism 101! Jesus loves the broken. This woman was broken, and her soul was hungry for the true Living Water, Jesus. Nothing in this life will satisfy soul hunger other than having a relationship with Jesus. The Samaritan woman at the well tried to bring satisfaction to her life with multiple men, but she still remained empty. You can try to fill your life with sex, people, money, and material possessions, but you will remain empty. Jesus is the Living Water, and anyone who hungers and thirst after Him will be filled. Jesus is intentional, and He is intentional about pursuing us in the depths of our disasters and even in our junk. He pursues us unrelentingly.

The apostle Paul speaks about how he wants to know Christ and the power of His resurrection and the participation in His suffering. Through our suffering, we are able to participate in Christ's crucifixion. We all want the blessing, but not many want to go through the pain of suffering or persecution to receive the blessing. The beauty of pain and suffering is that we get to share in what Jesus did on the Cross.

You might ask, "Why is going through pain and suffering good for us?"

Not only is there beauty in our suffering, but it draws us closer to Christ. Suffering strips away our self-reliance. Instead of looking within ourselves and to others for comfort; we will turn to God who is our Comforter. And through our suffering, we are changed more into the image of Christ.

I can remember a point in my life when I was going through some unprocessed pain, and I heard the Lord asking me, "Do you want to get well?" At one point I had gotten so used to pain in my life that I had learned to cope with it. Since I was a single mom, staying busy had become a coping mechanism for me.

However, coping with something is not truly dealing with the issue; it's more like putting a Band-aid over the wound, which enables to you to continue to function in life. Once the Band-aid comes off, you're again left with the effects of the pain because the wound never truly healed. I had been looking to certain people for help during this time, and the Lord began to slowly pull them away from me. My healing completely meant that I had to be willing to allow God to heal me—not seek help from people.

Please don't misunderstand what I am saying; I believe in seeking counsel. God does use counselors to bring about healing, and I will continue to use this method if need be. Unfortunately, we can look to people to help comfort us in our pain and forget that God is our ultimate Source for everything we need in life.

The lame man did not realize that someone greater than the pool was able to heal him, and His name is Jesus. Jesus is the greatest healer, and no one or nothing can heal, deliver, or set you free like He can. The man had not been healed by the waters in which he had placed his hopes year after year. In life, we can look to outside sources and place our hopes in people or, in this man's case, a pool of water. When will we learn that nothing or no one who can replace the ultimate Healer? God received the glory from this man's story.

III John 1 and 2 says, "I wish above all else that you will

prosper even as your soul prospers." As you are being healed in your soul, which is made up of your mind, your will and your emotions, you will start to prosper in every area of your life. That's why deliverance is good. Everyone needs deliverance, and you may even go through deliverance more than once; don't be ashamed if you need to. Deliverance is the children's bread.

When my brother was killed, the pain of losing him, as you can imagine, was very hard to process. I finally came to a point where I had to be patient with myself in the healing process. Yes, without a shadow of doubt, I knew my brother was in heaven. One day we will all see him again, and that knowledge gave me hope. But that understanding did not diminish the pain and grief that I had to work through. I had to come to a point where I wanted to get well and getting well required allowing Jesus to heal those areas where the pain was still real and raw. No one likes pain, and every person's response to painful situations is different.

We often hear people say that time heals all wounds, but the truth of the matter is time *with Jesus* heals all wounds. My question to you is: do you want to get well? Are you ready to allow Jesus in those areas that need to be healed so you can experience the abundant life that He has promised you? Friend, it's time to rise from that mat of pain and begin to walk into your freedom. All you have to do is open up to Him and allow

———

Him to heal those painful areas. Don't allow the Devil to make you ashamed of where and from what God has delivered you. You didn't go through what you've been through and come out of it simply to say you went through it. No, you went through a trial to testify of God's resurrection power in your life. You lived through your trial to help free others who are bound.

When referring to healing and deliverance, sometimes healing is not manifested right away; sometimes the person goes through a process because of that trial or circumstance. When Jesus healed some, He told them to go and show themselves to the priest; as they were following Jesus' instructions, their full healing was manifested (Luke 17:14). God's goal is not about how quickly He delivers you; rather, His goal is about the end result's looking more like Him.

---

1   "Grit," *Merriam-Webster.com*, https://www.merriam-webster.com/dictionary/grit, accessed 13 August 2019.

2   "Compassion," *Merriam-Webster.com*, https://www.merriam-webster.com/dictionary/grit, accessed 13 August 2019.

———

Questions

1) Like the lame man in this story, what has become your mat of comfort, so to speak?

2) What dream has God placed in your heart, but you have settled for less than what He has for you?

3) Are there any area(s) in your life where you need some accountability? Do you have people in your life who can speak into your life and therefore can hold you accountable?

4) What trial has God brought you out of that has not only refined you, but He wants to also get glory from your story?

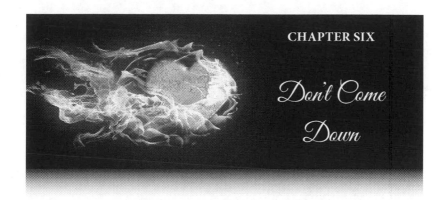

CHAPTER SIX

Don't Come Down

Sanballat and Gesham sent me this message: "Come, let us meet together in one of the villages on the plain of Ono." But they were scheming to harm me; ³so I sent messengers to them with this reply: "I am carrying on a great project and cannot go down. Why should the work stop while I leave it and go down to you?" – Nehemiah 6:2-3

NEHEMIAH WAS GIVEN the task of rebuilding the wall of Jerusalem after it was destroyed and burned by the Babylonians. When Nehemiah heard that the wall that once surrounded the city of Jerusalem had been broken down and burned, he wept (Nehemiah 1:3-4). Not only did the wall play an important part in the city's protection and security but also left the city defenseless and vulnerable to its enemies. Nehemiah spent some days praying and fasting before God (Nehemiah 1:4), and a burden was birthed in his heart. Before Nehemiah moved into action, he first sought God through prayer and fasting, asking God to grant him favor and mercy in the sight of the king whom he served as cupbearer. King Artaxerxes noticed that Nehemiah's downcast countenance since he had never before been sad in his presence (Nehemiah 2:1). The king recognized that Nehemiah's sadness was not ordinary but sadness from the heart (v. 2).

Those who served as cupbearers were trusted servants who made sure that the king's drinks weren't poisoned, as well as having the responsibility of bringing the king joy—not sadness. Despite Nehemiah's position as cupbearer to the king, he never forgot, first and foremost, he was accountable to the King of kings for his actions. The same holds true for every believer—no matter what our earthly title or position they may have, what matters is that they are doing the will of God.

After the king gave Nehemiah permission to be relieved from his duty as cupbearer, he left for Jerusalem. During his three-day stay, he inspected the wall during the night to prepare a strategy to get the work done (Nehemiah 2:11). Before you set out to do anything, sit down, count the cost, and consider what the work will take in time, energy, and resources. Don't be so quick to jump into something that you haven't truly counted the cost for the vision. Having a vision is good but having a strategy for working the vision is even better.

Nehemiah then shared the vision and what God placed on his heart to do with others who would be doing the work, and they all agreed to start rebuilding (Nehemiah 2:17). However, when they started rebuilding, Sanballat and Tobiah heard about what the Jews were doing and tried to stop the work through intimidation and ridicule (Nehemiah 2:19). Any time you set out to do anything for God, opposition will always come, and the greater the opposition, the greater the calling. The opposition proves that you are on the right track and that what you are doing will have an impact.

What is opposition? The *Merriam-Webster Online Dictionary* defines *opposition* as "hostile, contrary action or condition."[1] Let's face it, no one likes opposition! When we face opposition, we often want to wave our white flag of surrender and retreat, but the Scripture commands in Galatians 6:9 not to grow weary in well doing. The Enemy wouldn't waste his time fighting you if you were not a threat to his kingdom. The fact that he is hot on your trail proves that the work you are doing for God is causing damage to his kingdom.

Your assignment will always reveal your enemies. Any time you are fulfilling your assignment, your enemies will surface, so you must keep your focus on the Lord and remain in your position. As the building progressed, the threats intensified from ridicule to threats. However, Nehemiah would not stop the work to deal with the opposition. Instead, he sent a messenger with a reply to his enemies saying, "I am carrying on a great work, and I cannot come down" (Nehemiah 6:3). Nothing frustrates the Enemy more than when you completely ignore his tactics and maintain your focus on the Lord. What God has called you to do will require an "all-in" attitude.

Nehemiah knew the importance of being committed and focused. If he had chosen to leave the work and listen to his enemies, then the wall would not have been finished. Nehemiah had discernment in surmising his enemy's plans. When you are focused on God and what He has called you to do, you have no time to entertain the foolishness that comes to distract you from your assignment. Nehemiah shows us how to deal with opposition and overcome it. You cannot afford to be wishy-washy, double-minded, in today and out tomorrow. The opposition is sent to wear you down in hopes of making you quit.

In the process of writing this book, I have experienced opposition on every side, including my son's being involved in a car accident within months after having his first car, and having to move due to severe mold issues. I believe these attacks came to slow down my progress in writing, but I kept on writing. I was determined not to abandon the assignment because I knew this book was too important to quit writing.

As I have already mentioned, we are in a daily spiritual battle against our Adversary, and his tactics have not changed. At times, forgetting that our battle is spiritual and not about people is easy. People are not our enemy; rather, spiritual darkness is working in them. You must be discerning and see with spiritual eyes—not in the natural.

If you have ever seen a horse race, you likely would have noticed that the trainers attach what are called "blinders" to the bridle at the side of horse's eyes to help the horse focus his attention directly ahead. These blinders serve to keep the horse from being distracted by something from the side or behind him. Blinders are especially useful in running races.

In our Christian walk, we need to put on our spiritual blinders and remain focused on the things of God instead of being distracted by the Enemy. You cannot allow yourself to be pulled down by the distractions of the opposition, yet still maintain your focus on the things of God. Of course, some circumstances come to our life out of nowhere over which we have no control, but I am not referring to these instances. I am referring to choosing your battles wisely when dealing with opposition because most attacks are sent as distractions.

As the threats progressed, Nehemiah soon heard of his enemies' plan to attack and kill the builders. He then positioned men on the wall according to family to do the work of the Lord with their swords by their sides and their tools in their hands; they simply kept on working (Nehemiah 4:13). They successfully completed the wall because all worked together in unity to finish the project. They did not come down from their position; they stayed on the wall and kept building. The

Enemy will try to intimidate you through fear, slander, and false accusations, which are all smokescreens that he uses to persuade you to abandon your calling and assignment. The Enemy wants nothing more than to distract you and get you to throw in the towel. Hebrews 10:23 (KJV) instructs us to, *"hold fast the profession of our faith without wavering...."* Whatever your assignment is, refuse to stop doing the work of the Lord because of your enemies. Let your critics keep talking while you continue building and advancing the kingdom of God. The truth is if they were busy building and working, they wouldn't have time to focus on you.

Yes, we all know that dealing with the opposition can be tiresome, but when the attacks came to weary Nehemiah and the builders, he prayed that God would strengthen their hands to continue. I pray that as you continue to walk out this vision that God will strengthen your hands for the work to which He has called you. I pray you won't grow weary in well doing. I pray you won't lag behind or be delayed, but God will bring it about in His perfect timing.

I can tell you that when it comes to God's business, I am laser-focused on what I have to do. I know that distractions are sent to deter my focus from my assignment. I think we all can attest to procrastinating at times, but right now more than ever, we need be focused and determined to do whatever God has called us to do. It's time to put your hands to the plow while there is still time. John 9:4 says, *"As long as it is day, we must do the works of him who sent me. Night is coming, when no one can work."* Determine in your heart today that you will seek after God and all that He has called you to do.

Hold Your Position

Holding your position is a military tactic used as a method of warfare against the enemy that essentially means to stand your ground and not retreat during opposition.

> During combat, the military will send out the infantry unit first. The infantry or "foot soldiers" is the branch of an army that engages in military combat on foot. Foot soldiers have a much greater local situational awareness than other military forces due to their inherent intimate contact with the battlefield. A strong infantry is vital for taking or holding ground and securing battlefield victories.[2]

In spiritual terms, our position has very little to do with posture but everything to do with the principle on which our life is built and our ability to remain firmly fixed on the foundation of faith when adversity comes.[3] The Enemy knows the power, potential and promise of your position in the kingdom of God.

What is that position you may ask? Your position is in Christ and in the finished works of the Cross.[4] *"For no man can lay a foundation other than the one already laid, which is Jesus Christ"* (1 Corinthians 3:11). Jesus died on the cross and defeated hell and the grave; now He is seated in heaven at the right hand of the Father. He has given you the power and the keys to the kingdom of Heaven to bind and to loose (Matthew 16:19).

In the Bible, *keys* represent authority and power. When you have a key to something in the natural and the spiritual, you have been given authority and access to open and shut its door. *The Merriam-Webster Online Dictionary* says that one with authority has the power to determine or the right to delegate.[5] Our authority as a believer is in Christ, which means that a child of God has the power or the right to determine. Ephesians 1:19-21 says that power is the same as the mighty strength He exerted when He raised Christ from the dead and seated Him at His right hand in the heavenly realms, far above all rule and authority, power, and dominion and every name that is invoked, not only in the present age but also in the one to come.

If you have ever walked into a dark room where the atmosphere felt heavy and negative, you are being a light because you carry the Spirit of God within. Therefore, you have authority as a believer to shift the atmosphere with your presence and with your words.

Today, many Christians walk around with a defeated

mentality because they don't know who they are in Christ and the authority they have as a believer. God has given us dominion on earth, but when we don't know what this means, we walk around with a defeated mindset, allowing the Enemy to push us around. We have the power and authority given to us by Christ to overcome every attack against us. We must not accept defeat as our portion! We are children of God, and no weapon formed against us will prosper (Isaiah 54:17). One may form, but that weapon will not succeed against us.

The Word of God is the most powerful weapon we have as a believer. The Enemy knows the power of God's Word. In order to know our authority as believers, we must first know who we are in Christ. The Enemy is after our identity; he doesn't want us to know who we are in Christ. Knowing who we are is the most important revelation that we can have as a child of God. When we know who you are in Christ and the authority that you have in Him as a believer, you are able to stand firm in your position of authority. Only when we don't know who we are in Christ do we allow ourselves to be defeated by the attacks and lies of the Enemy. For that reason, we have the shield of faith in Ephesians 6:10 to quench every fiery dart of the Enemy.

When Jesus was in the wilderness and Satan tried to tempt him to forfeit his position and not go to the Cross, Jesus spoke, *"For it is written…."* He stood in His position of authority. God's Word has all power and authority over anything that the Enemy tries to throw at us. God's Word will stand for now and forevermore.

When faced with opposition, how do you respond? Do you cower under the attacks of the Enemy in defeat or do you stand in your authority as a believer? Jesus is our prime example of how to respond to opposition; He remained in His position of authority. When the religious leaders continuously tried to entrap Him with words, Jesus simply spoke and moved on. He already knew the motive behind their words and the intent of their hearts; therefore, He did not allow their personal attack to sidetrack Him and reduce Him to their level. He was always focused on the Father's business. Jesus warned His disciples that when personal attacks came to shake the dust off their feet and keep moving. Our progress is stopped every time we stop to fight a battle or settle a score. 2 Timothy 2:23 tells us not to have anything to do with foolish and stupid arguments because they produce quarrels.

Eagles are viewed as birds of great significance; in the bird kingdom, they soar high above the rest, living on the tops of mountains. In fact, the bald eagle was chosen as America's emblem because of its great strength, majesty, and the freedom this bird represents. We, the body of Christ, are like eagles because we are a royal priesthood; we have royalty in our DNA. When you know who you are in Christ, the less you will entertain the Enemy's lies. Have you ever seen an eagle stoop to the level of chickens, pecking at the ground for food? Never. Chickens can only see from a ground-level perspective while eagles were born to soar at great heights. The analogy I am trying to make is that when we choose to stoop to the Enemy's level, we are handing over our significance by choosing to believe what the Enemy is saying rather than what God says.

In other words, you don't have to respond to everything that people say about you. If what other people say about you can move you emotionally, then they can control you with their words. Choosing not to respond to what others say requires tremendous strength. Keep in mind that not everything deserves your attention or a response. Don't allow people to pull you down to their level. Don't let the opinions of what other people say about you make you doubt what God says about you.

Did you know that you have been positioned where you are for a reason? Could it be, like Esther, you have been positioned where you are for such a time as this? I know that you are divinely placed where you are for a purpose because God does nothing by happenstance. The book of Esther tells how she was placed in a position of influence during a time when culture did not value Jews, but especially women. Esther's uncle, Mordecai, realized that perhaps she had been positioned in the palace for a divine purpose—a purpose that could save her Jewish lineage.

"Do not think that because you are in the king's house you alone of all the Jews will escape. [14]For if you remain silent at this time, relief and deliverance for the Jews will arise from another place, but you and your father's family will perish. And who knows but that you have come to your royal position for such a time as this?" (Esther 4:13-14).

Christian women, you do have a voice! Like Esther, you are positioned on earth for such a time as this.

Joseph is yet another story of how a person can be raised from a place of obscurity to a place of influence, in order to save many lives, including his brothers who had betrayed him and sold him into slavery. Joseph told his brothers there was a purpose behind it all. *"Don't be afraid. Am I in the place of God? [20]You intended to harm me, but God intended it for good to accomplish what is now being done, the saving of many lives* (Genesis 50:19a-20).

God has you positioned right where you are for such a time as this. It may seem as if there is no significance in what you are doing now, but there is. You may not see it now, but God has a bigger purpose behind where you have been placed—whether it's at a secular job in the marketplace, the ministry, a place of business, being a stay-at-home mom or a janitor. That purpose is beyond what you can fathom. You have been strategically placed for such a time as this. Seeing your place in that light gives significance to what you are doing—even if what you are doing has become mundane or routine.

Wherever God sends you, you are supposed to take dominion over it, bringing God's kingdom into that place. As the church, we are the light and we should be in the forefront, influencing the world instead of the world's influencing us. However, we are now beginning to see the church in the forefront standing up and taking back its position of influence upon the seven mountains of culture, i.e., in business, media, education, government, entertainment, family and religion.

Our stand against injustice should never be about what's politically correct, but rather what's morally and biblically correct. It's about what's right and what's wrong—a battle between light and darkness. Our voice represents our authority and position. Whether you know it or not, your silence speaks. When we remain silent and refuse to speak out, we are turning a blind eye to the injustice, and we are equally as guilty as those who are committing the crime.

Great movements in history are marked by those who refused to conform to the ways of the world but stood in their position during adversity. During the Civil Rights movement, those such as Dr. Martin Luther King, Jr., and Rosa Parks chose to risk it all for the sake of seeing equality and equal rights for all races. We, the body of Christ, are called to confront matters of injustice. We have no right to pick and choose what issues we will confront while remaining silent on some of the others, all because we are afraid of ruffling people's feathers and making them uncomfortable within our sphere of influence. Taking this approach is actually cowardice.

Jesus was never afraid to confront social issues; He bridged gaps where cultural differences and backgrounds existed. Any injustice is wrong in the eyes of God and should be viewed that same way by us. Yes, abortion needs to be forbidden in our country, but we cannot address abortion without addressing *all* injustices including racism. Certain subject matters are basically addressed to the level of our comfort zone. What we seemingly refuse to confront we will not overcome. How are we reaching out to communities that don't look like us? I am not talking about reaching out only because that's what the Word of God says should be done; I am talking about really engaging and establishing relationships with those who do not look like us. Oftentimes the fear of the unknown holds us back from embracing people of other cultures and backgrounds. But the kingdom of God is multicultural and diverse. The time has come for believers to be repairers of the breach and begin to bridge gaps where racial and cultural tension exists.

True repentance is needed for all injustices starting from this generation going all the way back to Adam. When Nehemiah saw the state of Jerusalem and its brokenness, he wept. When was the last time, we, as the body of Christ, wept and repented over the sins of the world and injustices? Prayer was Nehemiah's starting point. He was so broken over the state of his country that it not only moved him to prayer, but also to action. For change to take place in our nation, prayer in the homes and the churches is the starting point.

> II Chronicles 7:14, *"If my people, who are called by name, will humble themselves and pray and seek my face and turn from their wicked ways, then I will hear from heaven, and I will forgive their sin and will heal their land."*

Our land will be healed when we earnestly seek the face of God and confront injustice. Refuse to allow the Enemy to muzzle your voice. Every voice is needed to put an end against abortion and racism. Through your voice, many will come into the kingdom of God, which is why the Enemy has been trying to silence you. You have a voice, and your voice carries weight and authority. *"And who knows but that you have come to your royal position for such a time as this?"* (Esther 4:14b).

AGAINST THE GRAIN

My dad would always tell us when we were growing up that any time we go against the grain or the norm of doing something we would not be liked. In other words, we would face opposition. Do you have a dream or a vision that goes against the grain that is outside the religious box or goes against the norm of doing things? If there's no blueprint or instructions for you to follow for the vision that God gave you, chances are you are a forerunner or a trailblazer.

A *forerunner*, according to the *Merriam-Webster Online Dictionary,* is "one who goes before in advance to announce the coming of someone or something that follows."[6] John the Baptist is an example of a forerunner in the Bible. He paved the way for the Jesus and the beginning of His ministry. As a forerunner, the path you are walking has no script, no blueprints or instructions to follow—uncharted territory, if you please. You are going ahead and paving a new path for others to follow. Yes, the cost is great, but so are the rewards for being obedient.

The story of Noah's building the ark comes to my mind when thinking of a prominent forerunner. Noah built something that no one had ever seen. When God told Noah to build the ark, he had no previous blueprints or instructions to follow—not to mention no one had ever heard of rain or seen a boat. I feel relatively sure that Noah questioned God. "Um, God, how am I going to build something that no one including me has never seen?" And God alone gave Noah the blueprint and the instructions, including the measurements and how to house all the animals. Talk about amazing!

If you are concerned about your vision and wondering how it will all happen, first of all, allow me to encourage you not to worry about the "how-to's" or the "what-to's." Simply keep doing what God told you to do. As you keep taking one step at a time, He will guide you every step of the way. Noah needed years to complete the ark, and as the years passed, I feel sure the pressure of quitting probably made more sense to him—not to mention the voices of his critics probably grew louder and louder as he progressed with building. If God has called you as a forerunner or a pioneer, you must be willing to stand for what you believe and not waver when the attacks come. Believe me, they will come! What will keep you going when all the voices of your critics are the loudest is seeing the vision birthed out. Lives will be forever changed, and souls will be won for the kingdom of God because you refused to quit, which is the primary reason why you keep plowing and charging ahead in the midst of opposition.

I once read a quote that said, "You have to be willing to believe in a dream that nobody else sees, but you." This quote describes the life of a forerunner or a pioneer. Doubt, fear and thoughts of giving up will try to hinder you from moving forward, but as a forerunner or a pioneer, you have to accept being misunderstood and criticized for what you carry.

Jesus operated outside the religious box, and many did not understand Him because some of what He did, like healing on the Sabbath, went against their religious system and laws. Jesus told the Pharisees that if they really knew Him, then they would know the work that He was doing. Since His critics did not know Him, they did not recognize His work. So many constrain the blessings of God in their lives, ministry, and business because whoever God sent to you did not come packaged in the way you expected. With a mindset like that, you will miss out on the moving of God all because a religious mindset won't let you see beyond what you are used to seeing and/or experiencing.

As a forerunner, be on guard against the religious spirit that will try to stifle the vision that God gave you. Religious mindsets won't understand because what God gave you is new and cutting edge; therefore, the religious crowd will criticize you for anything that looks completely different and goes against what they are used to seeing.

Newsflash! God will use whomever He wants to use or move however He wants to move. Who are we to say that God did not call a certain person or tell that person to do it a certain way? We have no right to try to put how God chooses to operate in a religious box. The best thing to do when we don't understand someone's assignment is to pray for them instead of criticizing what we don't understand.

When God has called you to birth a ministry or a business that is new and goes against the status quo of doing things, the hordes of hell will try to stop you from moving forward. Your number-one battle will be against the religious spirit in that region. Yes, you will be falsely accused for your assignment, but you must refuse to defend yourself. You have to understand that misunderstandings will come with the calling. They come with any ministry that will have a great impact for the kingdom of God. To those who don't understand, their assignment looks so different, Forerunners and pioneers are often looked upon as troublemakers or rebellious because what they are carrying looks different from the norm or the status quo.

Please don't misunderstand me. I am not talking about being in sin or out of order because we know we serve a God who does things in an orderly fashion. Rather, I am saying simply because someone does something that looks different or goes against the tradition of man does not mean the person is in error. God graced this person to be a forerunner. One of the reasons why forerunners become frustrated is because others try to make their vision fit someone's idea. Quit trying to make your vision fit the mold of someone else's vision! If God gave you a cutting-edge assignment, and no one has ever seen that assignment carried out in the way God instructed you, refuse to compromise for the sake of others misunderstanding you.

God knows some people need it the way He graced you to do it. Not everyone will understand your heart or assignment, but you are not here to convince people about your calling. You must give up your right to explain to others and trying to make them understand you because, seriously, explanations will only make the situation worse. Yes, people will try to place labels on you and even spread untruths. You must develop thick skin and realize what God says about you is what matters—not what people say about you. If what they are saying does not line up with the Word of God, then it's not from God. It's a lie from the pit of hell sent to make you doubt God and question what He told you. Don't take the bait! God is fortifying you through this process as you continue to stand.

I can remember a time when I came up against false accusations, and every time I tried to defend myself, the situation became even worse. Choosing to defend yourself when God wants to break you during this process is a form of pride. You must go through the process. Allow God to bring you to the point that you longer care about your reputation or what others say about you. Yes, this breaking is painful, but it's a part of suffering for Christ. Walking through all the false accusations was a very painful process for me. If you are walking through false accusations, trust God to vindicate you; refuse to defend yourself. God wants to teach you a lesson through all the false accusations and lies; that lesson is not to fear man and what others may what may say about you because fear can be a snare. Proverbs 29:25 says the fear of man is a snare, but whoever trusts in the Lord is kept safe.

If you care more about what people say, then they can manipulate you like a puppet. You'll be concerned about doing what they want you to do rather than what God has told you to do. Yes, false accusations are unfair, and they hurt deeply, but remember Jesus was falsely accused and He said not a word to His accusers. Yes, not defending yourself is a hard test, but God will vindicate you in His time. First, He will completely strip you of wanting to save your name and your reputation.

As a forerunner and pioneer, you must be willing to risk your reputation for the sake of what you carry, which is the Word of God. God wants to kill your inner feeling that wants affirmation and approval from man. If you are looking to others for validation and approval, you'll never fulfill the true calling of God on your life because you'll be easily swayed by what others think about you. You must endure what you are going through so you can show others that it can be done. That's why you cannot quit; you must defy the odds when everyone else expects you to buckle under the pressure. God will use every trial, every lie, and every false accusation being sent against you to teach you how to trust in Him alone. He will fortify you through this process.

Jesus told His disciples, *"For whoever wants to save their life will lose it, but whoever loses their life for me will find it"* (Matthew 16:25). In order to get to this place, I had to completely die to myself and my reputation. Getting to this place wasn't about what man was saying about me is that mattered, but knowing what God said about me. And I knew those words and labels had been sent as an assignment from the Enemy to make me quit my assignment. I knew God always held me in the palm of His hand, and no weapon formed against me prospered. He built me up and fortified me. He taught me that no one can stop the plans that He has for my life. If you are at this point in your life, allow God to deliver you from the approval of man. The quicker you come to terms with this, the quicker you'll move forward in your destiny.

As a forerunner, some of your greatest battles will be fought against familiarity and complacency, but you must continue plowing in order to embrace where God is leading you. As you continue to plow in the places that the soles of your feet may tread, God will give them to you. As you build, you are taking territory for the kingdom of God, and as you advance in that region, you will face opposition in the land sent to hinder the work God has assigned you from being carried out. But you will overcome the opposition as you continue plowing. God has sent you into that region as one of His foot soldiers. You will begin to root up and tear down territorial strongholds in that region. Yes, the battle will be wearisome, but the victory will be well worth it. Stay in position!

You might ask, "How do I know that what I am doing is of God?"

First of all, ask yourself if the assignment lines up with the Word of God. Does it bring glory to His name? Will it help to advance the kingdom of God? And most importantly, did you hear God's voice about the vision? All of these questions will help you stay focused when doubt and fear try to creep in and hinder you from going forward.

Just Do It!

I would guess that nearly everyone is familiar with Nike's slogan *Just Do It*. When God speaks to you to do a particular assignment, you don't owe anyone an explanation for your obedience to what God told you to do. Just do it! You don't need affirmation or approval from others in order to obey God. Just do it! If God spoke to you, then that's all the affirmation you need. *Just do it!*

Jesus' first miracle took place at a wedding ceremony when He turned water into wine. During that time period, serving the best wine first was a tradition; the family ran out of all their wine early. Mary, the mother of Jesus, intervened and asked

Jesus to help. She told the servants, "Do whatever He tells you" (John 2:5). The way the servants responded to Mary is the way we should respond to God's instructions—with prompt and complete obedience. We need to immediately lose the attitude, "I'll do it when I get around to it." Absolutely not! As a result of Jesus' intervention, the wedding guests commented that the host had saved the best wine for the conclusion of the wedding.

Our heart posture should always be "Lord, whatever You tell me to do, I will do it." I've heard it said that delayed obedience is disobedience. I surely don't want to walk in disobedience. When God speaks, every believer should be willing to promptly obey His instructions—no matter the cost. If God gave you a dream, then you must be willing to step out and take a risk. You cannot sit and wait for every detail to unfold before you start. Don't be afraid to make bold moves with God. Fear will try to stop you from moving forward with your dream, but you have to be willing to carry it out in fear and even when you don't have all the details.

Perhaps you stepped out before and failed. Now could be your time and your season to go back and redo the assignment. In Luke chapter 5, Peter toiled all day and night fishing but did not catch anything. Jesus called out to Peter, telling him, *"Put out into the deep water, and let down the nets for a catch"* (Luke 5:4b).

Simon [Peter] *answered, "Master, we've worked hard all*

night and haven't caught anything. But because you say so, I will let down the nets" (Luke 5:5).

Peter was basically saying that they had already tried once without success, but Jesus said to Peter, "Go back and do it again," and this time he would be successful. And as Peter obeyed Jesus' instruction, he caught a multitude of fish—so much so that the nets were breaking. You are one instruction away from unlocking your harvest.

Just like Peter, you may be saying, "God, I tried that already, and it didn't work for me." My friend, that plan may not have worked last year or last season, but *now* is your appointed time to step out on whatever God has told you to do! I don't believe that you missed God before; you were simply ahead of your time or your season, but your time and your season to go at it again has now arrived! Take a bold leap of faith. As you step out, your obedience will be rewarded. God's got your back, and He won't fail you!

One of my favorite quotes is by Thomas Edison who invented the light bulb after many failures. He said, "I have not failed. I simply found 10,000 ways that won't work." Perspective is everything. How you see yourself and the challenges you face determines your ability to overcome. Determination is the key driving force toward your goals. You must be willing to overcome your challenges.

May I leave a word of advice for you who are birthing a vision that is in the infancy stages of development? Be discerning of those with whom you share your vision. Don't allow anyone to manipulate you into sharing important information about your life with him or her, especially if your spirit is not at ease when spending time with this person. Some people who I call *dream killers* will try to kill what you carry. By all means, be careful to guard the vision and cover it in prayer. Don't let someone who has given up on his or her dreams talk you out of yours. No, I am not saying to live life distrusting everyone, but do pay attention to that check in your spirit about a certain person. The Holy Spirit doesn't lie. Some people have an agenda behind why they want to know certain things about you—especially intrusive folks, better known as *busybodies.*

My friend, you don't have time for busybodies! I try to use wisdom about what I share with others. Announcing everything that God has spoken to you with everyone who will listen is unwise. They cannot stop the promises of God for your life, but they can inflict unwarranted persecution and criticism on you. Some things are meant to be just between you and God. I have learned from experience that the gift of silence will bless your life.

Questions

1) What burden has God placed on your heart to do for Him? What are your passions? What calling do you believe God has placed on your heart?

2) How are you using your influence where you have been placed to advance the kingdom of God?

3) What and where has some opposition taken place regarding what God has called you to do? How did you respond to that opposition you faced?

4) Do you have a vision or dream that goes against the grain, so you're scared to step out in faith?

5) What actions steps and goals have you put in place to move forward with your vision?

---

1   "Opposition," Merriam-Webster.com, https://www.merriam-webster.com/dictionary/opposition, accessed 18 August 2019.

2   "Infantry," *Wikipedia*, 8 June 2019, https://en.wikipedia.org/wiki/infantry, accessed June 10, 2019.

———

3   L. Thomason, "Hold Your Position—A Devotion," November 22, 2011, *Wordpress.com*, https://lthomason.wordpress.com/2011/11/22/hold-your-position-a-devotion/, accessed June 10, 2019.

4   Ibid.

5   "Authority,"   *Merriam-Webster.com,*   https://www.merriam-webster.com/ dictionary/authority, accessed 18 August 2019.

6   "Forerunner,"   *Merriam-Webster.com,*   https://www.merriam-webster.com/ dictionary/forerunner, accessed 18 August 2019.

———

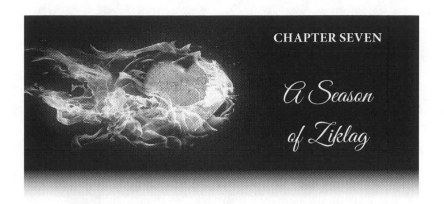

CHAPTER SEVEN

A Season of Ziklag

You Shall Recover All!

David and his men reached Ziklag on the third day, Now the Amalekites had raided the Negev and Ziklag, They had attacked Ziklag and burned it, ²and had taken captive the women and everyone else in it, both young and old. They killed none of them, but carried them off as they went their own way. – I Samuel 30:1-2

I N THE PREVIOUS chapter, David and the Israelite army had been battling against the Philistines. While the two nations were fighting, the Amalekites raided their base camp, carrying off the women and their possessions. Shocked by what he found upon returning to camp, David inquired of the Lord if he should pursue his enemies. *"Shall I pursue this raiding party? Will I overtake them?"* (1 Samuel 30:8a).

The Lord answered David, telling him to pursue them and

that he would overtake them and succeed in their rescue (1 Samuel 30:8b).

In our lifetime, I am sure we all have had "Ziklag seasons"—whatever that may mean to you. My idea of Ziklag seasons is where things that belonged to us—whether our health, our job, our immediate family, our joy or even our hope—were stolen from us. David never expected the enemy to invade their territory, and we never expect it either. The Enemy always attacks when we least expect it and when we are caught off guard. Like David and his men had some possessions stolen from them, we have too, but God wants to restore them to us. Also, like David who sought what had been stolen, we also have to seek what has been taken.

In David's moment of loss at Ziklag, what was considered his greatest loss became his greatest gain. The Scripture says in 1 Samuel 30:18-19 that David recovered everything the Amalekites had taken, including his two wives. Nothing was lacking or missing from the smallest to the greatest. They did not have to wait years to recover their losses. They recovered everything they had lost that same day plus more. David brought back everything. As a matter of fact, he and his men recovered so much and more that they had to give some of it away. Can somebody say, "Overflow!?"

We know that the Enemy is a thief, and his job is to steal, kill and destroy. When you know how he operates, the better you will be at discerning his tactics. Proverbs 6:31 says that when a thief is caught, he must pay *sevenfold*. That verse means that whatever the Enemy has stolen—whether it's your health, your finances, or your joy, it will be returned or multiplied back to you seven times. What I am trying to help you understand is not merely cliché; this directive is from the Word of God. David did not sit defeated and crying over his lost possessions; he sought the Lord and received approval to go after them.

The kingdom of God is not passive. The Word of God says that the kingdom of heaven suffers violence, and the violent take it back by force (Matthew 11:12). You can't simply sit twiddling your thumbs; you must become aggressive with the Enemy's advances. You must have boldness and a holy determination to take authority over the Devil and go after your assignment. Don't just sit there! Refuse to lay down in discouragement and defeat. You don't have time to sit and have a pity party over what you've lost. It's time to quit talking about all that the Enemy came in and took from you. The time has come to act. You must decide that you want back what was stolen from you. Think of it this way: would you allow a thief to come in and steal something as precious and as valuable to you as your child and carry him or her away while you sit still and watch? I don't think so! You would fight that thief with every fiber of your being to keep your child safe.

My favorite part of the movie *War Room* occurred when

Elizabeth Jordan, the character played by Priscilla Shirer, begin to stand up and take authority over the Enemy in her home and in her marriage. Elizabeth was already a warrior, but what she had on the inside of her had to be pulled out of her and trained how to fight spiritually. Taking a stand like Elizabeth Jordan did is exactly how we have to be when the Enemy invades our territory and takes what is rightfully ours. My friend, the time has come to take a stand! We serve a God of restoration, and God will restore whatever you've lost. I have no idea how that restoration will look for you, but I do know that God is faithful to His Word. He will restore to you the years that you have lost.

When Job went through a season of trials and testing, he lost absolutely everything—his health, his finances, his family, his possessions, and even the respect of his wife. Of course, from the natural aspect, things did not look good for Job, but Job's test became his greatest testimony. God not only restored everything that Job lost, but God gave him back "double for his trouble."

I am still standing and believing that God will continue to restore some things back to me, and I know He will. I want everything back that was stolen from me, but you know what? I had to be willing to do something about it and stop feeling sorry for myself. I had to get up from that position of feeling defeated and discouraged and go after what the Enemy had taken. God wanted to see if I was willing to take Him at His Word and go after what He promised.

I can testify that these seasons drew out the fighter in me. You have to get fed up with the Enemy and his taking what rightfully belongs to you season after season. You have to get fed up with being in lack year after year while everyone else is moving forward. His Word promises the following in Joel 2:25 and 26:

> "I will repay you for the years the locusts have eaten—the great locust and the young locust, the other locusts and the locust swarm—my great army that I sent among you. ²⁶You will have plenty to eat, until you are full, and you will praise the name of the LORD your God, who has worked wonders for you; never again will my people be shamed."

Farmers know all too well how locusts can decimate their crops, leaving nothing behind. Since they depend on their crops as their livelihood, locusts are an insidious threat to them. In this passage, the locusts represent the Enemy. They have the potential to devour a farmer's entire harvest before the crop can be harvested. In whatever area of your life the Enemy has devoured, God can and will restore it back to you.

The Bible testifies that Job was *"blameless and upright"* (Job 1:1). Job went through a season of testing—not because he had done something wrong—but for being faithful to the Lord. As a matter of fact, God *bragged* about Job's faithfulness. The Accuser of the brethren indicted Job of only being faithful to God because of His blessings on Job's life. *"But now stretch out your hand and strike everything he has, and he will surely curse you to your face"* (Job 1:11). God removed His hedge of protection from around Job and allowed him to be tested with only one stipulation: Satan could not take his life (Job 1:12).

We've all experienced things in our life that we felt were unfair and undeserving either to us personally or to a loved one. *"He causes his sun to rise on the evil and the good, and sends rain on the righteous and the unrighteous"* (Matthew 5:45). Storms of life, trials and seasons of adversity happen to all of us and being a child of God does not exempt anyone from experiencing loss; it's a natural part of life.

We have all experienced loss at some point in our life. If you are experiencing a Job-like season and you know you have been faithfully serving the Lord, have you considered the possibility that you could be going through a season of testing for being faithful? God asked Satan, *"Have you considered my servant Job?"* (Job 1:8a). Like Job, you may be going through this season because of what you are doing right and remaining faithful to God. Sure, Job had questions about why he was going through what he went through, but he came to the conclusion that he could trust God in the midst of his crisis.

We generally equate a season of testing with sin in our life, but that's not always the case. Yes, of course, examining our heart during these times is profitable; however, most seasons of testing come when we have been found faithful. Why? Because seasons of testing always pulls out what's really on the inside of our heart. Oftentimes, when we go through trials, we may begin to question God's goodness in our life, but only through the hard trials can we say, "God, I don't understand it all, but I will trust You." Job's season of testing brought him to the point of saying, *"Though his trial though he slay me, yet will I hope in him"* (Job 13:15a). Job knew that his season of suffering was allowed by God, and God alone knew the outcome and ultimately held the key to his life.

When a time of great testing comes to your life, look out because promotion is right around the corner. The test always comes before the promotion. Joseph was tested in the pit before he was promoted to the palace. No test = no promotion. We all like being promoted but not being tested.

I can attest to enduring seasons of loss where what I gained spiritually far outweighed my losses or anything of material value during those seasons. I grew closer to the Lord and learned to trust Him at a much deeper level than I did before the trial. I can attest that I have seen the hand of God repeatedly protecting and shielding me from the snares of the Enemy. You may be experiencing what seems like a Job season; the Enemy has viciously attacked you from every side. May I encourage you not to give up? From personal experience, I can say that it gets darkest right before your greatest breakthrough!

When Job came out of his season of testing, he inherited a double portion. He gained far more than what he had started with! I don't know about you, but I am standing in faith for my double-portion return from what I've lost while remaining faithful. I will stand in agreement with you as well that God will restore to you what has been stolen.

The Scripture says that Job inherited a double portion when he prayed for his friends. This Scripture holds one of the keys to inheriting that double portion. In other words, praying for those who persecute you, walking in forgiveness, and showing love toward those who have hurt us captures the heart of the Father. Can you stand in the gap for others to receive their miracle or breakthrough while you are still standing, believing for yours?

Job's so-called friends weren't very comforting during his season of hardship. They came to "comfort" him by seeing if he had sinned against God as the cause of his suffering! Job described his friends as *"miserable comforters"* (Job 16:2). Have you ever been around some folks who try your patience to the point you want to give them a piece of your mind, but the

Holy Ghost won't let you? I am sure this is what Job's friends must have been like. But after Job prayed for his *"miserable comforters,"* I mean his friends, God restored what he had lost and gave him twice as much as he once had (Job 42:10). Job's restoration reveals the heart of God. When you can pray for and bless your enemies, God brings about restoration to that area in your life; it will be better than it was before. God is not a duplicator, and neither is He a replicator; He is the originator, and He makes all things new!

In I Samuel 30:6 the men talked about stoning David because of their tremendous grief. In spite of their anger and disappointment, David found a way to encourage himself in the Lord. David did not look for someone else to encourage him; neither did he sit stewing in his anger and frustration about his losses. Instead, David encouraged himself in the Lord.

When life throws one of its most devastating blows toward you, encouraging yourself can indeed be difficult. At times, my friend, encouraging yourself in the Lord is exactly what you must learn to do. Yes, having people in our life who can encourage us when we are down is good, and nothing is wrong with having friends who are encouragers. However, when no one is around to encourage you through your storm or when times come like David faced when everyone turned their backs on him, what will you do?

Can you encourage yourself through these tough times? I

am sure David probably had a flashback over his life when God had rescued and had delivered him during times of difficulty. I feel relatively sure that he remembered the times of running and hiding from King Saul and how God had hidden him and protected him from Saul's vengeful pursuit. As you can imagine, this attack from his own followers came at a time when he was weary from a battle. Did you know during times of weariness is generally when the Enemy attacks us with his greatest assaults? Our defenses are down, and our discernment is lessened, but thankfully, David found a way to encourage himself in the Lord.

How many of us can say that when we are going through one of our greatest seasons of loss that we can strengthen ourselves in the Lord like David did? I am not talking about putting on a smile and pretending like everything is good; rather, I am referring to truly being able to encourage yourself in the Lord. In all honesty, I faced seasons that I couldn't encourage myself, and I didn't know how to because I was at such a low place in my life. I found it hard to even come out of the depression and discouragement that had set into my life. But despite what seasons we go through, God is good. What we are going through does not change who God is and His love for us.

When I realize that I am going through a low point in my life, I begin to recall to memory all that the Lord has brought me through and His faithfulness. His goodness and mercy will pursue us all the days of our lives—even when things are not going so well. We serve a God who is good, and His nature does not change when our circumstances do.

I have learned when we are going through a difficult time, we will find Him closer to us than before. *"The LORD is close to the brokenhearted and saves those who are crushed in spirit"* (Psalm 34:18). All we need to do is call upon His name, and He will comfort us. My friend, if you are in a similar season, simply begin to recall all that the Lord has brought you through. Thank Him for not only bringing you out of your circumstance but for bringing you through it.

The Bible says in I Samuel 30:9 that David had a total of six hundred men who served with him, but only four hundred continued the pursuit with David. The other two hundred remained behind because they were too exhausted to cross the valley (v. 10). Right before your biggest breakthrough, you will likely be tempted to give up and throw in the towel as these 200 men did. You will battle weariness and discouragement on every side. The times when we are at a point where it seems as if we can't take another step forward, that's when our greatest breakthrough is right around the corner. I often wonder if God would have strengthened them from the journey—if only they had taken the next step.

The Enemy wants you to give up and quit when you are at the very brink of your breakthrough. This is when the Enemy will fight you the hardest, but the blessing is in the pressing forward. As you continue to press through all the opposition and not quit, you will see the victory on the other side of this battle. I would like to encourage you to strap up those boot laces and hold your position, child of God! You've come too far to quit now.

As David pursued his enemies and did not give up, God gave David the supernatural ability to overcome them. God did not give David a five-step action plan to overcome his enemies; He simply told David to pursue them, and in David's obedience, God He gave him the assurance that he would able to overcome his enemies and recover everything. The same will be true for you: in your pursuit to regain and recover what was stolen, you will begin to see restoration take place.

When you are facing perilous times in your life, when you are at your wit's end, and when you don't have any strength left in you, that's when God supernaturally steps in on your behalf. When you have come to the end of your rope, that's when you see God move on your behalf. This does not imply that God was not there all along; rather, it means that when you've exhausted all your human efforts of trying to do it within yourself, that's when God steps in with heavenly assistance. When He does, He then receives the glory. For when we are weak, He is strong. You don't need to try to do things in your own strength. Honestly, you can try, but you won't get very far. Only by the grace of God and His mercy have I made it this far. I can share stories in my life that I know only God carried me through because the proof is in my testimony. I know what He has delivered me from and brought me through, and He alone receives the glory!

When David received his share of plunder, he did not exclude the two hundred men simply because they were too exhausted to continue. The Scripture says that when David and his men approached the two hundred, *"he asked them how they were"* (1 Samuel 30:21b).

But all the evil men and troublemakers among David's followers said, "Because they did not go out with us, we will not share with them the plunder we recovered" (v. 22).

David stepped in, negated their selfish plans, and ordered, *"The share of the man who stayed with the supplies is to be the same as that of him who went down to the battle. All will share alike"* (v. 24b).

David could have easily sided with the other men and kept the plunder, but he understood always doing what is right to others—especially those who had helped along the way—is most important. Some people will always try to eliminate others, but God is the rewarder. I feel relatively sure those two hundred men probably felt discouraged and disappointed at the time because they couldn't continue with David.

The future king of Israel demonstrated not only what true leadership looks like, but also being Christ-like. God blesses us so that we can be a blessing to others. We will have people in our lives who help us along the way in our journey. Some will continue with us for the long haul or they will be short-term sprinters in our journey. It doesn't matter! Go back and bless them for being a part of your life. I have friends who have stood unswervingly with me during the tests of time for years, and there are some I only talk to occasionally. Both groups of friends are equally important to me. Always take notice of those who have your best interests at heart, and make it known to them how much you appreciate and value their friendship.

In leadership, knowing what others are capable of is good—especially those you lead. We must be careful of putting certain expectations on those who do not have the mental or spiritual capacity for certain tasks. The Bible instructs us to know those who labor among us. I am sure David knew his men very well. We all have moments of weaknesses in our journey. Sometimes those who want to continue with us in the journey or battle have good intentions, but they have become too weary to continue for whatever reason. Their inability to continue does not mean we should toss them to the side. No, we must come alongside of them and allow them to regain their strength so that they can get back in the game and continue to run their race.

We fail to realize that God is a rewarder, and He does not look down on us when we fail or quit for whatever reason. He knows what He placed on the inside of us, and He knows how much we can handle. The fact is, the burden is not for us to handle; it's for us to give to Him. I promise you; God can carry your burden.

It's Already Yours!

In Joshua 18:1-3, the entire assembly of the Israelites had gathered at Shiloh and had erected a tent for meeting. The country had been brought under their control, but seven Israelite tribes still had not yet received their inheritance. Five tribes had already taken their portion of land that Moses had given them according to tribe. *So Joshua said to the remaining Israelites: "How long will you wait before you begin to take possession of the land that the* LORD, *the God of your ancestors, has given you?"* (v. 3). In other words, Joshua was asking them what they were waiting on. He was asking, "Why are you still sitting here?" The land was already theirs; all they had to do is go in and occupy it.

Sometimes we can be so proactive about matters in our life, but we can be so lazy when it comes to the things of God. We begin to think everything is simply supposed to fall into our lap without putting in any work or effort on our part. If you are honest with yourself, you can agree to a certain degree with my conjecture. Yes, all the promises of God belong to you; this is your inheritance in Christ; however, you must understand that you take possession of what is already yours in Christ by faith.

If you are lacking peace in your life, then you already know that through Christ that peace is yours. It's already available for you!

We can be like the seven tribes who just sat still and allowed complacency to rob them of what already belonged to them— simply because they were not willing to take possession of what was already theirs. My friend, we are not called to be complacent Christians!

Joshua is trying to encourage the remaining seven tribes to take possession of the land that God had already given to them. We can develop this same mentality to where we simply go through the motions of life without having any aspirations or goals to want to do more with our life. We know what God has already promised us, but we must be willing to go after what He already said we can have.

The seven tribes were simply sitting on the sidelines, chilling and waiting for their portion of land to fall into their laps. I have news for them and you; it's not going to fall into your lap! If you want what God has for you, you have to be willing to go after it. Even though God had told the Israelites that He was giving them the land of Canaan, that promise did not mean the people would not have to put forth some effort and fight for the land. You cannot be lazy in the kingdom of God. God had said if they were willing and obedient, then He would give them the land. As they were willing to go in and fight for the land, God gave their enemies over to them one by one. If you make a mental picture of this scenario, the enemies of the Israelites were basically "squatting" on their property. Each tribe had to go in and serve eviction notices to their enemies. I am saying to you, "It's time for you to serve the Devil an eviction notice and begin to take back what belongs to you!"

I am sure you have heard the phrase that actions speak louder than words. You can tell so much about someone through his or her actions. As the saying goes, talk is cheap, but what are you willing to do? Some Christians are not willing to fight for what belongs to them because they don't want to engage in spiritual warfare. God loves fighters and those who take Him at His Word. He took me, a natural fighter, and turned me into a warrior for His kingdom. When it's time to go to battle and fight, I'm in—all in. He knows that I am not afraid to fight the Enemy. Now is the time to rise up out of the land of not enough, to go in, to take possession, and to occupy the land of more than enough that God already has for you.

Get in Where You Fit In

Too often I see many Christians falling into the "comparison trap." Comparing ourselves with each other is so unwise. *"We do not dare to classify or compare ourselves with some who commend themselves. When they measure themselves by themselves and compare themselves with themselves, they are not wise"* (2 Corinthians 10:12). When we compare ourselves to others, we don't know our true identity, how this action takes away our authenticity, and who God called us to be.

If you try to be someone else or model yourself after someone, you are doing yourself a disservice and robbing others of what you have to offer. My friend, we women are the worst about comparison, and I can speak from experience. At one point in my life, I too fell into this trap. I believe I can say most of us at some point in our life have fallen into this trap. And a trap is exactly what comparison is. Comparison is a trap that we fall into, thinking that we are not good enough to be our true authentic self. We sell ourselves short when we try to be something we are not. Sure, we will have people in our life we admire and wish to emulate, but we should never try to fashion our life after that person. God created you exactly how He wanted to create you with your unique personality—quirks and all.

You are called to reach certain people that I am not and cannot, so they need you to be who God designed and created you to be. You won't have an effective influence where God has placed you if you are not being who God created and designed you to be. I am definitely an introvert, but depending on the setting, I can also be an extrovert. If you are an introvert, you definitely understand what I am saying. The struggle is real; let me tell you. I find it amazing how God uses me and my personality in various ways. I've learned to get out of His way and let Him lead me wherever He desires.

When David tried on Saul's armor for his fight with Goliath, it was too big for the future king, nor was he able to prove the weaponry. David removed Saul's armor and decided to use his familiar weapons—a slingshot and some smooth stones—to defeat Goliath. I am sure that Saul had good intentions in trying to help David; however, our good intentions could possibly hinder someone else in his or her walk with God. *Nobody can be you.* God did not create you to be a carbon copy of someone else. He created you to be your own unique and authentic self, and that's exactly who the world needs to see.

Sometimes a leader has to be careful when seeing the potential in others and attempting to mold them into a certain personality. Our so-called *polishing* could take away who they really are. We cannot fit them into a certain mold to suit our specifications because of how we want them to look or act. I always tell people that I am a bit rough around the edges, so don't try to categorize me; you'll find yourself frustrated because I'm a "mold breaker." Be who God created and called you to be! If being you offends others, that attitude has nothing to do with you; it's insecurity on their part because they don't have the courage to be real.

The Devil's lie is we can't be real and vulnerable because we think that people will be disappointed with seeing the real and authentic side of us. However, the world needs to see the real you. I think that we wear so many hats in life that we can lose ourselves in the process of trying to please everybody. God never called us to be people pleasers—only to please Him. Our aim is not to please man, but to please God. We must let our hearts and minds be set on pleasing God first and foremost; then He gives us favor with those we are around.

IT'S IN YOUR ASKING!

In 2 Kings 2, Elisha had been following and serving Elijah, his mentor. Elijah knew that he was going to be taken by God, and before his departing, the man of God said to Elisha, *"Tell me, what can I do for you before I am taken from you?"* (v. 9b).

"Let me inherit a double portion of your spirit," Elisha replied (v. 9c). Indeed, God honored Elisha's request and grants him a double portion of Elijah's spirit. The Scripture records that Elisha did twice as many miracles as his mentor Elijah. We serve a great God, and nothing is too hard for Him; however, we often limit God in our asking. Oftentimes, we are afraid to ask God because we either doubt that He will come through for us or we think that our asking for big things is too hard for God to fulfill.

The truth is, there are times when we don't know how to ask God for big things. God is waiting for us to believe Him for the impossible. He is waiting for us to ask Him for things that only He can perform. God gets the glory out of our lives when He does things that no man could have possibly done. He wants us to have a crazy audacious faith in Him. We serve a God who created the heavens and the earth, so why are we so afraid to ask Him for big things? He stretches our faith to ask Him for the crazy big requests. We must start thinking and asking on a greater level, and I am not thinking only about material possessions. We can apply this truth spiritually as well. Elisha asked for the double portion of Elijah's anointing, which he received. We can ask God for the same, but make sure you are prepared and ready for what you are asking.

What you desire from God is in your asking. The Word of God says in Matthew 7:7, *"Ask and it will be given to you; seek and you will find; knock and the door will be opened to you."* One way to receive that for which you are asking is to be specific in your asking and then don't doubt. When you ask, you must believe because the one who doubts is like a wave of the sea, blown and tossed by the wind (James 1:6). God already knows what you need or desire, but He still wants you to ask Him. What if Elisha had remained quiet and dismissed the notion to ask? Simple! He would have never received his double portion. This story is in the Bible for a reason, and that reason is because God wants to stretch you in the way you think and what you are asking from Him. Don't settle for less than God's best for you. We rob ourselves and sell ourselves short when we do so.

Sometimes what we may be asking from God can be seen as difficult—even to those who may have been in the faith longer than we have. Elijah told Elisha that what he was asking was *a difficult thing* (2 Kings 2:10). Elijah knew that this was something that only God Himself could fulfill for his protégé. When you have crazy faith to believe Him, you will hear from the skeptics. Don't be surprised when it's those who have walked the Christian walk longer than you have. That is why God loves and honors childlike faith. If God has been trying to stretch your faith in asking Him for big things that only He can do, that's an open invitation! My friend, don't hold back; you'll be amazed at when you look back. All you will say is "Look at God"! He wants to show up and show out for His children. And He deserves to do exactly that because we serve a big God!

Questions

1) What are some area(s) in your life where you are believing God for complete restoration?

2) What are some Scriptures on which you are actively standing while in your season of Ziklag?

3) What are some things that God has already spoken to you about and you've been sitting on the sidelines instead of stepping out in faith?

4) Have you ever allowed the "comparison trap" of others to rob you of uniqueness in Christ? When and what have you done to change that paradigm since then?

5) Has God ever stretched your faith to ask Him for big things that only He can do? If so, what has been the result of your asking?

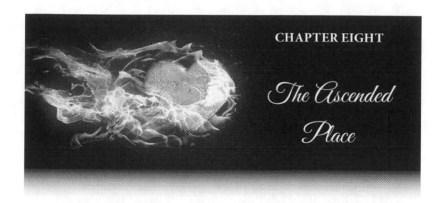

CHAPTER EIGHT

The Ascended Place

And the LORD said to Moses, "I will do the very thing you have asked, because I am pleased with you and I know you by name," Then Moses said, "Now show me your glory" (Exodus 33:17-18).

T HE ASCENDED PLACE is a place of meeting with God—the place where we go to encounter His presence. According to the *Cambridge English Online Dictionary*, the word *ascended* means "to move, climb, or go upward, to rise at a higher point."[1] This place could be your prayer closet or it could be in your car as you drive to work or your local church. Nothing is special about the place itself, but what makes it special is having an encounter with God. When we encounter God, our life is changed.

Moses had an encounter with God at the burning bush, and his encounter changed his life forever. When you truly have an encounter with God, your life will never be the same; it will be transformational. You can never go back to your old self. As a matter of fact, you won't have any desire to go back. When you've encountered His presence, you are no longer satisfied with what's considered *normal* Christianity.

In the Old Testament, the glory of God appeared as a pillar of cloud that would come down and stay at the entrance of the tent of meeting (Exodus 33:9). This presence is called the *kabod*, which means "heavyweight" or "the weighty presence of God."[2] In the Old Testament, the presence of God went before the children of Israel and led them out of Egypt with a pillar of cloud by day and fire by night. Exodus 34:29 says that every time Moses came down from Mount Sinai, his face was radiant because he had spoken with the Lord.

A Christian who has been in the presence of the Lord is marked with the radiance of His glory. We no longer have to look for the glory of God as in Old Testament times; rather, we carry His glory on the inside of us when we come to know Christ as our Savior. The glory of God is revealed through us by the Spirit of God.

The Bible says that we go from glory to glory, which means that we are continually being changed into the image of God. In His presence there is the fullness of joy, as well as healing and deliverance. In His presence, there is peace. Being in His presence brings extraordinary benefits. Psalms 91:1 (KJV) speaks of being in "the secret place." *"He that dwelleth in the secret place of the most High shall rest under the shadow of the*

Almighty." The word *dwell* means "to remain."[3] When we enter into the secret place, we will experience rest in His presence. I can tell you that nothing is like being in the presence of God. Jeremiah 33:3 says, *"Call to me and I will answer you and tell you great and unsearchable things you do not know."* How do you come to know about His plans for your life? By being in His presence and remaining in the secret place, communing with God. The believer finds revelation in His presence.

In Matthew 16:15, Jesus asked Peter, "Who do you say that I am?"

Peter replied that Jesus was the Messiah, the Son of the living God.

Jesus told Peter that this was only revealed to him by the Father in Heaven (Matthew 16:17). In other words, there is revelation in the presence of God. Jesus was asking, "Peter, do you know Me for yourself?" Jesus' question was not addressing what Peter had heard others say about his Master, but did he know Jesus for himself.

Now the question for you is this: do you know Him for yourself? Do you only have information or head knowledge about who Jesus is or have you had an encounter with Him that changed your life? Have you encountered His presence? When you truly know Him and have had an encounter with Him for yourself, no one can convince you otherwise.

I can testify that I know Him in so many ways throughout

my Christian walk. I know Him as my Savior, as my Provider, as my Healer, as my Deliverer, and as my Comforter. I can go on and on because He has been all of these things and more in my life. I can tell you that I did not merely have some religious experience; I had an encounter with the Living God, and I know Him for myself. He's not someone I only read about in the Bible; He has walked with me through so many seasons that He is undeniably real to me.

LEVEL UP!

I have already mentioned the eagle is one of my favorite birds. Not only was the eagle chosen as our great nation's symbol, but the Bible mentions the eagle several times. The eagle is known for its ability to soar at great heights. When a storm is coming, the eagle will use the winds from the storm to help propel it above the storm. They love to soar above the clouds because of the clearer view at this height. We can learn many lessons from the eagle's ways. When we are going through the storms of life, we can choose to soar above the storm and see the way God sees them.

Sometimes we can become blinded by our current circumstance because we are directly in the midst and have only a nearsighted view of the issues. We cannot see any other perspective but ours because we are face to face with the situation. When we step aside and begin to ask God for

His perspective, we begin to have a clearer view of what is happening. As we see things through the lenses of Christ, we come to learn that our situation is not as it always appears. Sure, you may be in the thick of that situation and you can't see your way out of it but choose to remain focused on God. His ways and thoughts are higher than ours. He can see things beyond our scope of view. When you have God's perspective, you are like the eagle that flies above the storm so that it can have a clearer view.

Your perspective is changed at a higher elevation; therefore, God is calling you to a higher level with Him. If you've ever climbed a steep mountain, you probably noticed that the higher you climb the clearer the air is. Your vision is so broad you can see for miles. God wants His children to ascend to the top of the mountain like Moses so that we can experience a greater level of intimacy with Him. He has so much more for us; therefore, we must keep our focus on Him. He wants us to see from His perspective and through His eyes. As long as you remain on ground level so to speak, you will view life from that perspective.

Have you ever flown on an airplane and experienced turbulence? If so, you know how absolutely scary it can be. You are thousands of feet in the air, and you have no control over what the atmosphere is doing. All kinds of thoughts begin to race through your mind. The pilot will sometimes make an announcement regarding the turbulence, but even with his calm assurance, you remain afraid. However, the pilot will still have to fly through the turbulence in order to come out of the storm.

When we are going through turbulent times, we often cannot see our way out of them. You can feel scary and a bit shaky, and you want to be out of the situation as quickly as possible, but God knows how to get you through it. We can't see on the other side of the storm, but when God is piloting your life, He knows how to bring you through. We maintain God's perspective by choosing to have our mind and heart set on things that are above. The Enemy does not want us to have God's perspective; he wants to keep us at ground level right in the middle of chaos where you won't have any peace. When this chaos happens, many times you will begin to focus on the problem more than you are on Jesus.

I can remember going through a situation, and God told me that it wasn't the way that it appeared. The issue seemed that way to me because I was so focused on what I was going through. I was right smack in the middle of this chaos, and that was all I could focus on. Finally, I took time to step back from the situation and asked God to help me to see it His way. He showed me the truth. I realized that I had become so focused on this issue that I had taken my eyes off Him, which made what I was going through much bigger than it seemed.

In the grand scheme of things, I created a mountain out of a molehill—all because of how I chose to view the situation. We tend to do that when we don't have God's perspective and tend not to see the bigger picture behind what's really happening. I am so grateful that I serve a God who will help adjust our lenses when we get out of focus. *He does. Every. Single. Time.*

The Enemy loves to fight for our focus. We know protecting our focus is a daily battle. One of the ways the Enemy can get us to take our focus off Jesus is through the offense. The term *friendly fire* is a military term when someone from your team or forces begin to fire at each other.[4] The spirit of offense is one of the primary ways that the Enemy uses to bait Christians against one another. His goal is bring strife and division. Today, too much offense is going on—especially in the body of Christ. We tend to allow the Enemy to get us offended at every little issue. If he can get us offended at each other, there's no unity, which hinders your walk with the Lord and quenches the Holy Spirit. Think of offense like a dam that can hinder and hold you back from the things of God, including His blessings being released in your life.

When offense comes knocking, slam the door shut; don't even entertain the notion. I am sure we have plenty of things to be offended by, but it is not worth the trouble. You have too much work to do for the kingdom of God then to allow offense to hold you back from all that God has for you. Be especially careful when you are trying to guard your heart against offense. The Enemy is so sneaky he will employ someone you love who has been offended to bring an offense to you. You can side with the person you love. Taking on someone else's offense is dangerous, and opening the door for offense to take root in your heart because you love the person who is being hurt.

Many times I've seen others take on someone else's offense all because of their affiliation with the person. Be careful when cases like this crop up, for this is very dangerous. Allowing the views of others to be shaped and influenced by what others say is carnal. Your assumptions of someone can be completely off base. Before you make assumptions about a person, truly get to know that person for yourself—not based on someone else's experience or judgment. When someone is offended at a person, how he or she views that person is affected adversely. The body of Christ should be so rooted in love that we are able to disarm the Enemy when someone brings offense to our door. I can only speak from experience because I have been on both sides of the door of this entrapment devised by the Enemy to hinder you.

Keep in mind that the Enemy will try to bring up every offensive thought to the memory in order to keep you offended. As a child of God, don't entertain the thoughts of offense; use the Word of God as your weapon to pull down anything that the Enemy tries to whisper in your ear. Just like the eagle, you will have to choose to soar above offense; don't take the bait. You might think, *this is easier said than done!* At times, that assumption can be true, but you must choose not to be offended. The way we see things in the natural affects how we see things spiritually. What we see and how we see matters will affect our heart; therefore, having the right perspective is so important.

David cried out to God, *"Create in me a clean heart, O God; and renew a right spirit within me"* (Psalm 51:10 KJV). Our hearts and mind can become defiled by that which we see, hear or encounter, which is why it is so important to guard our heart for out of the heart flows the issues of life. That which you focus on will have an impact on how you view things in life. If you focus on the negative, then the negative will flow out of your mouth. *"For out of the abundance of the heart the mouth speaketh"* (Matthew 12:34b KJV).

The Upper Room

After Jesus' ascension, in the starting of the early church, the disciples came together daily to pray in an upstairs room while they waited on the gift of the Holy Spirit. As they all came together in one place, a mighty rushing wind suddenly filled the whole house, and tongues of fire came to rest on each of them. As they all were filled with the Holy Spirit, they began to speak in other tongues (Acts 2:1-4). This event was the birthing of the new church.

In the Old Testament, God told Moses to build Him a sanctuary where He could dwell among the people. The Old Testament sanctuary was a structure which consisted of the outer court, the altar of sacrifice (the bronze altar), and the tabernacle itself was divided into two chambers. The first chamber was the Holy Place and only the priest was allowed to enter into this section; the second chamber was called the Holy of Holies. The structure of the tabernacle was in the Old Testament, but Christians now have something better than the Old Testament tabernacle. We have the Spirit of God dwelling within us. I am so glad that we are under the New Covenant which is under grace and not law. *"I would not have known what sin was had it not been for the law"* (Romans 7:7b).

In the Old Testament, the priest's duty involved keeping the fire burning on the altar day and night. We keep the fire of God burning in our lives through prayer, which is the most powerful weapon children of God possess. Can you imagine how much work was needed in keeping up the tabernacle and offering burnt sacrifices for sins? Praise God, we don't have to burn and sacrifice animals for our sins! We have something better than burnt sacrifices—Jesus Christ! Jesus died on the cross and paid the ultimate sacrifice for our sins. The children of Israel asked Moses to intercede on their behalf because they were afraid to approach God. We don't have to be afraid; we can come boldly to the throne of grace.

Jesus is our greatest Intercessor and is constantly interceding on our behalf night and day. No longer is there any separation between God and us. When Christ died on the cross, the veil that separated Him from us was torn from top to bottom. We are no longer separated by a veil, but through the blood of Jesus, we have access to enter into the Holy of Holies. His children can boldly approach the throne of grace at any time. The only separation is on our behalf, and that's if you are afraid or don't want Him, but He denies no one who humbly comes before Him.

It saddens me to hear about Christians who are afraid to pray or think that their prayers are not good enough to be heard or that some other Christian prayers are more powerful or more effective than theirs. This concept is a deception. God loves to hear the simplest of prayers, and He hears the silent ones too. At times all you can get out is "God, help me!" He also hears and answers that prayer too. You don't have to be a skilled prayer warrior for God to answer your prayers. Simply speak to Him from your heart; that's what He is looking for. Prayer does not have to be deep. Be real with God by expressing your heart and concerns to Him. Don't think that prayer is supposed to be in some kind of format such as the King James language. It doesn't because prayer is simply talking to God.

The key to developing a prayer life is to remain consistent. Take baby steps and start out with praying five minutes a day and then gradually increase that time. As you remain consistent, you'll start developing a love and a passion for prayer. Sooner or later those five minutes will extend beyond that five minutes, and you won't worry about the time. Instead, you'll be consumed with being in His presence; time won't matter to you.

THE PROMISED GLORY

"I will shake all nations, and what is desired by all nations will come, and I will fill this house with glory," says the LORD Almighty. "The glory of this present house will be greater than the glory of the former house" (Haggai 2:7, 9). We, the church, is about to see the greatest move of the Holy Spirit on the earth. I believe this move of the Holy Spirit will usher in the greatest revival that will touch every nation on this earth. We will begin to see the *church* (the true houses of God) being filled to overflowing with the harvest of souls. I believe a thick tangible presence of the glory of God will be seen like never before. We are getting ready for an end-times revival which will bring in millions of souls for the kingdom of God.

As the church begins to get serious about prayer and seeking the face of God, we have to position ourselves so as not to be so restricted by time and programs. We need to allow the Holy Spirit to move freely. I believe God is preparing the body of Christ now for a deeper level of consecration before Him. He is calling us back to consecration so that He can prepare our hearts for what is getting ready to take place on earth. I believe the glory in the house of God will be so thick that it will appear as if there will be a fire. But this fire—the fire of God—will begin to cleanse and purify anything that is not like Him. He will consume and burn up the idols at the altars and any strange fire.

God is preparing the hearts of His people for the glory that will manifest in the new house. We always know that God is doing a new thing, and that is even true with His house. We are being fashioned and prepared for the coming glory that will manifest upon true houses of God, i.e., those who have prepared for His glory to rest. We prepare by setting our spiritual houses and the house of God in order. I believe that when the church becomes serious about prayer and hungers after the things of God, we will see revivals igniting all over.

When we hear the word *revival*, we often equate the term with known revivals such as the Azusa Street and Brownsville revivals, but I believe this soon coming revival will not be accredited to any man. God will not share His glory with anyone. A revival causes a ripple effect of what first ignites in our own lives through prayer and consecration and spreads like wildfire, igniting everything in its path and setting those ablaze who are hungry for more of God.

Exodus 33:11 says that when Moses returned to the camp, *"his young aide Joshua son of Nun did not leave the tent."* He remained in the glory of God even after Moses had left the tent of meeting. Glory carriers, who are seekers of His presence, love being in the presence of God; they are consumed with being in His presence.

Our youth today is the "Joshua generation"—a generation of bold worshipers who love being in the presence of God. I absolutely love going to Christian conferences and seeing how the younger generation love being in the presence of God. When you think of all the things that they could be doing or involved in the world, that they choose to be in the presence of God is miraculous! Their hunger after the things of God is so amazing to witness. There's no earthly comparison; it's truly amazing to encounter God.

1   "Ascended," *CambridgeDictionaries.com* https://dictionary.cambridge.org/us/dictionary/english/ascend? q=ascended+, accessed 13 August 2019.

2   *"kabod,"* BibleHub.com, https://biblehub.com/hebrew/3519b.htm, accessed 13 August 2019.

3   "Dwell," *Merriam-Webster.com,* http://www.merriam-webster.com/dictionary/dwell, accessed 13 August 2019.

4   "Friendly fire," *Merriam-Webster.com,* http://www.merriam-Webster.com/dictionary/friendly%20fire.

Questions

1) Do you have a place where you can go and encounter the presence of God on a regular basis?

2) How has being in His presence marked you or changed you for His glory?

3) In what way(s) has God caused you to "level up," meaning how has He been challenging you to change your perspective about any situation and how has this "leveling up" shaped your spiritual walk?

4) Do you have a consistent prayer life? If not, identify those issues that may be hindering your prayer time. Once you have identified these hindrances, how can you increase your prayer time?

A Prayer of Deliverance

My testimony of living with shame after having an abortion

I was 21 years old when I underwent the abortion of my first child. For years, I lived with so much shame and regret. Abortion wounds a person's soul. BUT JESUS IS THE HEALER. He will come in and heal every wounded area in your heart and soul. All you have to do is let Him in. Not everyone's healing happens in the same way. Some are healed instantly. Some healing happens in layers and seasons of time. Some can be healed while attending a church service, during a healing conference, or while sitting at home. God is not limited in the way He can heal a hurting person. I have learned that you must be patient with yourself but keep seeking Jesus for complete wholeness.

If you've ever had an abortion or if you were the one who initiated the abortion either for your girlfriend, friend, or family member, please consider the following:

First of all, I want you to know that Jesus loves you so very much! The reason why you had the abortion doesn't matter and is a moot point. Right now, lay it at His feet. You cannot

———

carry this shame any longer. Jesus died so that you wouldn't have to carry it. Regardless of what you have done, Jesus still loves YOU! Nothing can separate you from the love of Jesus! He pursues you, and right now, He's reaching out to you with open arms.

I want to help walk you through your waiting deliverance.

- First, repent. If you haven't repented, you need to repent right now of having an abortion.
- Second, you must forgive yourself. God cannot forgive you until you forgive yourself. We expose every lie of the Enemy who has said you are unworthy. My friend, you are so worthy!
- Third, you must forgive and pray for all those who were involved in the abortion procedure—the doctors, the nurses, those who attended you, etc. Pray that they will repent and come to know the truth.

For years even after I was saved, I still held onto the fact that I had undergone an abortion. Yes, I knew that my sins were forgiven, but at times I still longed for my unborn child. Of course, the Enemy will try to come at you with shame and condemnation, but there is no condemnation for those that are in Christ Jesus. Jesus does not shame or condemn you.

So right now, we expose the Enemy who will try to tell you

———

that you are unworthy and will try to get you to hold onto this heartache.

> *Right now, God, I release the Devil's lie and give it to You. Right now, I want You to heal this deep wound with Your love. Holy Spirit, please come in right now and fill that wound with Your power. In Jesus' name, Amen.*

You may say, "Well, I had an abortion, but I've forgiven myself years ago for that." I did too, but I still felt a longing for my unborn child that kept me bound for years.

> *So right now, I break the attachment that has kept me bound and longing for my unborn child. I break off the shame and condemnation. I expose every lie that says I am unloved. Make me free right now in Jesus' name. Right now, I break off the shame I feel. I dismantle and expose every lie from the Enemy that has held me in bondage to my past. Jesus, wrap Your arms of love around me right now.*

If you ever had an abortion or know someone who has and you need prayer, please feel free to contact me. And if you think you need further deliverance, reach out to your local church or a church that operates in deliverance that can walk you through further deliverance. There is no shame in needing more deliverance. God's deliverance is for you.

A Prayer of Salvation

While you were yet a sinner, Christ died for you. While you were still in your mess or going through your mess, Christ died for you. I don't care where you are now or once were; Christ died for YOU! You don't have to wait until you think you are ready or have it all together before you come to Jesus. The truth is that none of us have it all together, and without Christ, we are all a disaster. He is calling you and pursuing you from the depths of your mess into His loving arms.

There is no other way to heaven than through the name Jesus. His is the name that is above all names. He is standing now at the door, waiting. Will you open the door of your heart and let Him come in? If so, read the following verse, and then say the prayer out loud from your heart.

> Romans 10:9-10, *If you declare with your mouth, "Jesus is Lord," and believe in your heart that God raised him from the dead, you will be saved.* *¹⁰For it is with your heart that you believe and*

———

*are justified, and it is with your mouth that you
profess your faith and are saved.*

Jesus, I admit that I am a sinner. I ask that
You forgive me for all my sins. I believe that You
are the Son of God, that You died on the cross
for my sins, and You rose from the grave. I want
to follow You all the days of my life. I ask that
You come into my heart as my Lord and Savior.
In Jesus' name. Amen.

If you said this prayer and meant it in your heart,
congratulations and welcome to the family of God! Please
contact me at <u>chavonda@compassionfire.com</u> or you can write
to me at: PO Box 50571, Knoxville, Tennessee 37950 to let
me know that you made this decision for salvation. I want to
celebrate your decision with you!

Get ready! I promise that your life will never be the same!

———

Printed in the United States
By Bookmasters